SKILLS FOR THOUGHTFUL THOUGHT

Notes

KIMBERLY GOARD PH.D.

Kendall Hunt
publishing company

Kendall Hunt
publishing company

www.kendallhunt.com
Send all inquiries to:
4050 Westmark Drive
Dubuque, IA 52004-1840

Table of Contents

FINDING THE TRUTH

TOOLS FOR THINKING WELL

Prologue to Skills and Virtues for Thoughtful Thought

Right now, you are thinking. This is a book about thinking. Many people don't think about their thinking, and much less do they read a book about it.

But if you stop and consider what's important to you as a human being living in a world where you are being sent messages by
    all different types of people
    and corporations
    and special interest groups
    and governments,
you might conclude that thinking for yourself is vital.

You are not a robot merely accepting data that is given to you, right? Do you know that you have the freedom (and responsibility) to make choices about what to do and what to believe? Do you realize that it is your job as a human to try to believe as little falsity as possible? If you've never thought about this before, now is the time to step up and take control of your thought life. You are neither a robot who has been pre-programmed nor a sponge who must soak up and accept every bit of information that comes your way without evaluating it first. In fact, your mind is very special and it should be treated as such. Just as you wouldn't want a dump truck to pour trash into the sunroof of your new car, you shouldn't want rubbish to fill your mind either.

If you are tempted to say that your mind isn't anything unique or special, I can understand why. You do share many of the same mental features with everyone else who has a mind and who is a human being. But the fact that any of us human beings have a mind at all is a very special thing!

Our minds allow us to do many amazing things. Without the minds that we have, humans would not be able to
    add,
    divide,
    do mathematical proofs,
    write algorithms,
    create computer programs,
    enjoy poetry,
    diagnose a medical problem,
    create and prescribe medicines to treat health problems.

> Human minds are amazing and they separate us from other living things. Thus, they are worth developing so our lives as humans can flourish.

Without our minds, we would not be able to
read or write novels,
create music,
have intricate and nuanced ways of communicating with one another,
figure out the best way to engineer a roadway or building,
deny our impulses,
keep up the quality of a product while trying to contain the costs it takes to make it.

Further, without our minds, we would not be able to
resist urges to do things we consider to be bad,
make ourselves do things that we don't want to do but we know we should,
make plans and set goals,
weigh our options,
communicate well with others who think differently from us,
and many other valuable things.

Since our mind is so important, we should make sure we use it to the best of our ability. Many things go into doing this, but you must start somewhere. This book will provide some encouragement for you to think about how to exercise the parts of your mind that allow you to think critically and form better beliefs. The main goal of this book is to help us grasp Truth more clearly.

This is a book about how to think well. Like many other valuable things, thinking—if it is to be done well—must be thought about and trained. You must think about thinking to do it well; you must practice good intellectual habits. Some types of mental activity do not require thought and practice, as they naturally and properly occur properly. For example, unless there is something wrong, you can breathe without thinking about it. Your heart beats without you consciously telling it to beat. While many things seem to be dependent on the functioning of our brain, not all mental activity needs to be observed, evaluated, and trained. But as we form important beliefs, make important decisions, and decide what's true and what's false, we need intellectual skills and virtues.

If you were asked to think of something to tell me about, you may pause for a moment and then recall a funny story, or you may reflect on an embarrassing memory. You may proclaim your preference for cold weather over hot weather, or you may imagine something you and I plan to do together soon. In each of these scenarios, you are thinking. Your brain experiences lots of activity, and most of it occurs without you being aware of it. Sometimes we are unaware of what we think or believe about a particular subject. Sometimes we may experience an emotion but not realize that we are feeling it until someone asks us why we seem so sad or angry or happy. Our brains help us detect and process so many internal and external stimuli. Some of it is conscious, and some is unconscious or subconscious. While all forms of mental activity are important, this book will focus on CRITICAL thinking. (You will learn all about this means in Chapter 1.)

If you want your thinking to be clear, helpful, and deep, you have to think about how to think well and you must train your thoughts to be this way. While thinking is central to your life, thinking well is not always easy. In part, thinking well means recognizing that your emotions are important but shouldn't dominate your thoughts. Thoughts and emotions are often intertwined, but you can distinguish thinking from feeling, so you must not equate them. Instead, you should be aware of each and determine the role that each should have in your decision-making. Another part of thinking well means learning to insert calm and logical thoughts into the process that culminates in an action. Your thoughts and actions are often intertwined,

> If you want your thinking to be clear and helpful and deep, you have to train your thoughts to be this way!

but they are not equivalent. Thinking before you act is sometimes necessary if you are going to do the right thing. Thinking well means that you have recognized and corrected unhelpful patterns of thought that, when evaluated objectively, do not leave you with a greater glimpse of Truth and Reality. Thinking well also means that the inferences that you make are logical rather than illogical.

> Thoughts and beliefs may be held personally, but they are not private.
> They affect what we do in public.

Training yourself to think clearly, logically, deeply, and efficiently will enhance your life. Your thoughts affect so many aspects of your life, so you need to make sure that you are thinking well. This book will introduce you to some skills and virtues that will help you become a better thinker. After reading this book and practicing the skills it encourages, you will likely recognize that you can develop these skills further. Becoming a better thinker can be a life-long goal. But this book will set you on the path to improvement and will offer you basic skills that will increase your ability to think well and to think critically.

One thing you may begin to notice as you go through this book is that critical thinkers have the potential to be better communicators. There are a lot of critical thinking skills that can be applied to personal situations or those with a group dynamic. In this book, we will explore some ways to think clearly, evaluate our own thinking and the thought of others, and some ways to communicate with people more effectively.

Critical thinking will provide benefits to everyone in many facets of life—in the relationships you have, in your personal thought life, and almost every profession! One reason that this is true is because the thoughts that you have affect the things you do. What you think will often be reflected in what you say, in the way you treat people, in the goals that you have, in the decisions you make, and in the things that you value. The things that you do now and the choices that you make today will affect your life in the future. Our goal should be to flourish as human beings in the context of our community, so we need to choose our actions wisely.

Let's consider the following beliefs and attitudes and their corresponding actions:

Example #1:
   Belief: You think that hardened criminals do not deserve basic, human rights.
   Possible action or inaction: You verbally support a warden who forces violent criminals to have brain surgeries, which will make them more docile, even though the prisoners do not agree to the surgery.
   Possible action or inaction: You happen to work as a security guard, and you don't mind getting extra rough or denying food to the prisoners whom you don't like.

Example #2:
   Belief: You believe that people's health is important, and you are thankful that you have had pretty good health over your lifetime.
   Possible action or inaction: You notice that someone in your hometown is lobbying to get a low-cost healthcare clinic in your town, so you go out of your way to sign it.
   Possible action or inaction: You decide to pursue a degree in the healthcare field.
   Possible action or inaction: You join a gym and do strenuous activity 6 days per week.

Example #3:
   Belief: Family is very important and children are a blessing.
   Possible action or inaction: You skip a major exam in one of your classes because your sister is feeling nauseous and you don't want to leave her by herself.
   Possible action or inaction: You intend to have several children and will only marry a spouse who also wants a big family.

As you can see, many of the beliefs and thoughts that we have are connected to the things we do or refrain from doing. In a way, thoughts, beliefs, and attitudes are a public matter. While we view them as personal, they reflect who we are publicly. Their power to impact our public actions does not permit them to be exclusively private.

This book will present you with the opportunity to become more intellectually virtuous, less biased, more precise, and more logical. In essence, it will help you be a better thinker so that you can make more disciplined and authentic choices concerning your life and can more skillfully flourish as a human.

Why Should We Care About Learning To Think Critically?

You will likely find many reasons to care about becoming a better critical thinker as you go through this book. At this point, I will mention a few of the benefits, without trying to convince you of them. Critical thinking can help improve your life in several ways. It can help you get to know yourself better. It can help you recognize your patterns of thought so that you can choose to think in the best way possible. It will help you detect an increased number of options in life situations. It will enhance your discernment of what is true from what is merely fictional. It will help you be persuaded by things of substance and value rather than by hype or emotionalism. It will allow you, then, to make more authentic choices that you truly wish to make, rather than making choices based on what you think other people want you to make. It also can help you become more articulate and persuasive. Critical thinking liberates us to make independent decisions that are authentic and genuine.

Since people's thought lives affect our actions, we need to become clear and rational thinkers. This will enable us, potentially, to make better ethical choices and it will aid us in making decisions when an answer isn't obvious. Critical thinking will strengthen the mind of the person thinking. A mind must be used and it will atrophy over time unless it is exercised. Critical thinking will help the brain grow and reorganize itself, even in most adults.

Of course, just because someone famous says something, it does not make it true. Nevertheless, we are wise to consider the beliefs and thoughts of great thinkers. Many famous intellectuals suggest that we should care about thinking. I think they are right, but if you do not yet agree, please continue to read through this book with an open mind and see if critical thinking skills benefit your life. I hope that this book will open your eyes to the worthwhile benefits of critical thinking and the impact that these skills can have on your life.

A Note about Learning

If you haven't already, you should begin to think of yourself as an instrument for learning. Begin thinking of yourself as a questioner. Begin thinking of yourself as a problem solver. You already are these things, but this book will help you hone these skills so you will be able to do them at a higher level. In the end, you may not be able to solve every moral dilemma or math problem that you encounter. Your English grammar may not improve that much because of this book. You certainly won't learn how to trade stocks and become a millionaire and won't turn into a concert pianist. However, you will have honed some basic thinking skills and attitudes that are very likely to contribute to your success in these areas, if you choose to apply yourself in them. But if this isn't "your thing," you will still be much more able to read closely, analyze what people say, think of substantial questions, respond to new experiences in a better way, take charge of your learning, be skeptical of the right things, be more mentally grounded in reality, write more clearly, and support your viewpoints.

Life is a series of developmental stages—physical, emotional, and personal. Our intellect, our views, and what we learn, experience, and believe are no different. People also go through stages of thinking and learning. No matter what your stage, this book can help you achieve the next level.

One Tip for Enhanced Success

When you encounter questions that are asked within the chapters, discipline yourself to answer the questions before reading more. You do not necessarily have to write out the answer, although some people can work out their thoughts much easier if they write them out. There will also be "Practice" and "Apply" questions. Use these to make you think about the concepts that have been presented. Doing this *before* looking up the answers at the end of the book will enhance your understanding and will help you develop critical thinking skills.

What's Special about This Book?

The author of this book believes:

- most of what is true exists externally to human minds, and that wisdom, in part, comes from learning more about and respecting Truth more fully.

  Thus, I make a distinction between subjectivity and objectivity but recognize the importance of equipping students to navigate the areas between the two.

- solid epistemological principles should undergird our belief-formation process.

  Thus, I have included a section that provides principles about the proper justification of beliefs.

- having a foundational vocabulary is important to learning a subject.

  Thus, the book introduces vocabulary for each topic and does so in an accessible way.

- clarity is important in teaching.

  Thus, I have tried to explain concepts and procedures simply without glossing over the logical connections among ideas.

- someone is more motivated to learn if she sees why the topic can be helpful.

  Thus, I explain the importance or relevance of topics.

- intellectual and moral virtues are vital to a flourishing human life.

  Thus, I devote a chapter to intellectual virtues and I ask students to apply them to their attitudes, actions, and skills as the book progresses.

- education has the power to shape a person's attitudes as well as their skills.

  Thus, in addition to several practice assessments, I allow the reader to reflect on and assess his beliefs and attitudes, and I regularly encourage meta-cognition, (thinking about what and how you are thinking.)

- the human mind is special and deserving of respect.

  Thus, I write of human dignity and respect for oneself and others, as well as for their arguments.

- each person is ultimately responsible for his education.

  Thus, I remind students of their responsibility to take ownership of the learning process and to see themselves as rational beings with minds worth developing.

- education in all disciplines merges to give a greater understanding of one Reality.

  Thus, I make references to music, art, science, medicine, history, and other disciplines and I ask questions that will encourage a synthesis of skills they develop as they progress through the book.

- students are more likely to read and remember if they are presented with a mixture of stories and content.

  Thus, I have written prose and straightforward information.

The book not only teaches about intellectual skills, but it helps you practice these skills. It asks questions where readers must define terms appropriately, compare and contrast different beliefs, manipulate statements while preserving their truth value, and make valid rudimentary inferences. Readers are prompted to defend their positions and to consider how to express their beliefs well in the context of other people and our society. The book encourages its readers to be intellectually virtuous in a more systematic way in the future, avoiding unfair biases and informal fallacies, while having the ultimate goal of seeking the Truth.

Acknowledgements

I am grateful for the opportunity to write this book. There are many people who have suffered through my summer writing process without me being as present as I would have preferred. Specifically, I am thankful to my mom, husband, and son for allowing me to have divided attention during this project.

I want to thank three other people who have given me specific encouragement. Dr. Angie Adams-Smoot imparted to me the idea to write this text. L. J. Brown gave me early feedback on three chapters, as well as helpful suggestions and encouragement. Dr. Pamela Case read through every chapter of my manuscript, gave me great ideas in each one of them, but prevented me from making a couple of significant blunders in two of them.

Thank you to my team at Kendall Hunt, especially Chrissy DeWitt for wanting to work with me despite my forthrightness and hesitation. I also appreciate Katie Celarek who has been good at answering each of my mundane technical questions.

Author Bio

Dr. Kimberly Goard holds a Ph.D. in Philosophy from the University of Kentucky, an M.A. in Humanities from the University of Louisville, a B.S. in Philosophy and Religious Studies from Radford University, and a B.A. in Economics, concentrating in Health Care Administration, from Roanoke College. She is the author of *Unconditional Forgivingness*. Goard is an Associate Professor of Philosophy, department chairperson, and the Chorus director for Richmond Community College in North Carolina. She also teaches a master's level class in the Classical Pedagogy of Philosophy for Classical Conversations. A native of Virginia, she now resides in Pinehurst, NC.

Chapter 1
The Value and Skills of Critical Thinking

1.1 Introduction

In this chapter, you will be introduced to several basic terms and will think about thinking in a way that you may not have thought about before. You will also learn to distinguish between regular and critical thinking. Make sure you become familiar with each of the examples of critical thinking skills because you should apply them to situations you'll encounter in life and in this book. Knowing the difference between subjectivity and objectivity will be especially helpful and will give you a great context for knowing the difference among facts, reasoned judgment, and opinions. Also in this chapter, you will learn about three basic and logical rules that have persisted since ancient times and are so foundational that they undergird everything in this book.

1.2 Terms to Know

Critical thinker: Someone who uses a set of skills and habits to help evaluate reasoning, detect and solve problems, and discover truths. Critical thinkers don't just accept everything that is told to them. Instead, they analyze, think in depth about pros and cons, compare and contrast concepts, evaluate information, and try to be logical and unbiased as they apply standards and draw conclusions from the evidence that is presented to them.

Proposition: The meaning held within a statement (i.e., a declarative sentence).

Truth value: The quality a proposition has when it, at least in theory, can be judged as true or as false.

Objective: Separate from a person's desires, beliefs, and biases. It is based in Reality and Truth, apart from a person's perception of it.

Subjective: Dependent on a person's desires, beliefs, and biases.

Personal standards: Standards that we believe to be true and may be more or less objective, depending on the nature of the topic and our criteria for accepting the belief.

Logic: The branch of philosophy that studies reasoning and prescribes what makes sense.

Fact: A well-supported and generally accepted statement that is thought by a majority of people to be true.

Opinion: A subjective view about a topic that does not connect us to the truth or falsity of an objective Reality.

Reasoned judgment: A classification of issues or beliefs about which there is no obviously accepted truth, but that has truth value and is accompanied by relevant knowledge and evidence.

Law of non-contradiction: the logical rule that states that a proposition cannot be both true and false at the same time when referring to the same thing

Law of identity: the principle that something is what it is; it is not something other than what it is.

Law of excluded middle: the principle that maintains that a statement cannot be something between true and false. No simple statement that is properly qualified falls between truth and falsity.

1.3 Skills

1.3.1 Why We Must Train to Think Critically

Your mind exists, in part, so that you can gather information and use it productively. Your mind empowers you to take charge of your emotions and your intellectual life. But your mind has to be trained. People cannot develop their intellectual abilities if they have no idea what their intellect is or what it might be able to do if it trained several of its abilities. For most human beings, the following analogy holds: Just as we are born with a talent—for example, to make people laugh, to be a fast runner, to sing along so well with the radio that people don't ask us to be quiet, or to season your cooking well—we are born with the ability to think critically. But if the person who has the talent never watches other comedians, never develops his leg muscles and cardiovascular system, never exercises his vocal cords, and refuses to cook, then this talent will never be developed to its full capacity. In some way, the person's life will be diminished from what it should be. Similarly, if we do not develop our critical thinking skills, our minds will not be able to realize their potential.

Critical thinking is part of what it means for a person to live well in the world. As you read this book, your mind will be training itself to make greater sense of the world. Your critical thinking skills will help your mind become better at constructing new, useful knowledge that will not only be especially helpful to your life goals but will also connect you to reality in a greater way.

This process of developing your critical thinking skills, however, can't be completed in one semester. You can develop and strengthen your critical thinking skills in new ways and in new situations for years to come. While you will, hopefully, learn a lot from this book, you should also plan to use these skills in all different settings, including in your classes, your career, your family life, and developing your worldview.

> **Critical thinker:** Someone who uses a set of physiological skills and habits to help evaluate reasoning, detect and solve problems, and discover truths. Critical thinkers don't just accept everything that is told to them. Instead, they analyze, think in depth about pros and cons, compare and contrast concepts, evaluate information, and try to be logical and unbiased as they apply standards and draw conclusions from the evidence that is presented to them.

Regular Thinking

Critical thinking is a special form of thinking. It is not merely regular thinking. Regular thinking doesn't usually take much effort. If you are thinking regularly, you may let your mind wander and you may accept the things that naturally come into your mind as you daydream, watch television, or notice the things around you while you take a walk. Regular thinking tends to be reactionary and easily affected by emotions. While on a walk, if you see a cat dart out from under a bush, you may get startled and then say to yourself, "That's just a cat." If you see an injured bird on the sidewalk, you may feel slightly sad. These observations and reactions are typical of basic thinking. We must do this kind of thinking every day. But many times, life requires that we think harder and deeper about things. It requires that we think *critically*.

Critical Thinking

What is critical thinking? One definition is that it is the thinking that is done when you use intellectual and psychological skills to evaluate reasoning, detect and solve problems, and discover the truth. A more detailed definition of critical thinking skills is "a complex weave of abilities that help you get someone's point, generate reasons for your own point, evaluate the reasons given by others, decide what to do or what not to do, decide what information to accept or reject, explain a complicated idea, apply conscious quality control as you think, and resist propaganda."[i]

To think critically, we must adopt a certain attitude and stance toward knowledge, our emotions, other people, and how we interpret the world. We must try to separate what is true from what we merely think is true. We must be aware of our biases or mistaken assumptions and try not to let those affect our decision-making. We should be willing to assess whether we should hold the views and beliefs that we hold.

Critical thinking involves separating yourself from common biases when making decisions and judgments. This type of thinking, when done well, involves being logical and using several virtues (which will be discussed later in this book) to help us think well and beyond the surface-level thinking that we regularly do. Critical thinkers usually evaluate the ideas that are presented to them before accepting them. They judge the quality of data that is given in support of ideas or theories before believing it. They look for loopholes or counterarguments to what they say so that they can fix potential problems in their thinking so that the views they hold are more likely to be correct. Critical thinkers try to be clear and consistent, and they try to say and think of things that are important rather than frivolous. Further, they try to be organized and fair.

The "critical" part of critical thinking does not have to do with criticizing people or their views. A critical thinker does not need to be mean or irritable to think critically. You will see in this book that thinking critically and communicating well often involves deciding how to be kind to people so that they can properly respect your views. "Critical," as it relates to "critical thinking," is derived from the Greek word, *kritikos* (pronounced krit-ee-kos), which means something like "skilled in judging." If you would like to be more equipped to judge information, views, controversial claims, beliefs, and many other things, this is the right book for you!

Eight Critical Thinking Skills

Multiple skills can be listed as examples of critical thinking. One such list includes analyzing, judging with standards, discriminating, assessing and using information wisely, information seeking, logical reasoning, weighing the pros and cons, transforming knowledge, and being clear and precise.[ii] Let's consider each item in this list as well as what it might look like in practice:

---

1. Analyzing

An example of analyzing a concept: A parent is frustrated with the repeated disobedience of her child, Max. As an act of discipline, she takes the child's texting privilege away for one week. The child says, "That's not fair." The mother asks what "fair" means. To answer the question, the concept of fairness would have to be defined. One definition of fairness means "giving people what is due to them." Another definition of fairness is "to treat people or situations that are very similar as being similar, and to treat people or situations that are very different as if they are different in those ways." The two definitions of fairness have been distinguished so the concept of "fair" is clearer to both people. (Notice that other aspects of this situation could be analyzed.)

- Begin with a whole unit of something—whether it's a problematic situation or a concept. Then, separate it into logical units that can be studied and compared, distinguishing things that are different.

- Begin with a group of data or statements and generalize them into simple statements or theories that account for much of the information they contain.

- Begin with someone's beliefs or views and logically think of the ramifications of the view, what goes into the view, identify the assumptions inherent in the view, and contrast it to other similar concepts.

---

2. Judging with Objective Standards

An example of judging with objective standards: Refer to the example above concerning analyzing the concept of fairness. After the concept is defined, in this case in two different ways, the mother and child can use the definition as a rule or standard by which to measure the mother's disciplinary action. They can ask, "Does denying a child the privilege of texting his friends deny him something due to him?" The simple answer would be "no," since texting friends as a past-time is not a right but is something that can be done sometimes in the proper circumstances.

- Using the rules of conduct or expectations established by a professional group, or logical necessity, decide whether a specific act meets the expectations.
- Using standards of a genre of art or music, or some other rule, evaluate a performance, piece, or item.

3. Discriminating

An example of discrimination occurs when the mother has to answer Max's protests that his friends still get to text, so he should get to as well. Discrimination takes place as the mother points out the differences in the situation. She says, "Yes, many of them can text, however, they are not my son or daughter and I'm not in charge of them. Furthermore, the circumstances have changed from how things normally are because of your disobedience. There are consequences to your actions and you have now entered a time where you can no longer have this privilege."

- Recognize differences and similarities among things or situations.
- Place things into different or overlapping categories as needed.

4. Gathering, Assessing, and Using Information Wisely

An example of using information wisely is seen when Max's mother answers the following objection. Max says, "You are still being unfair to me, and to Scott, my best friend. His parents had invited me to go to the pool with them this afternoon and they are waiting on a response about whether I can go." With this new information, the mother chooses to let the son text his friend briefly to say that he cannot go to the pool today and that he will likely be unable to text for the coming week. This response allows the mother to maintain fairness and respect for other people, yet it maintains the discipline she intends to uphold.

- Before accepting what someone says, consider whether you are being given all the relevant information.
- Look for evidence and facts before making important decisions or evaluations.
- Carefully adjudicate between reliable and unfairly biased or otherwise unreliable information sources.
- Consider both sides to an issue rather than only focusing on what you already think.

5. Logical Reasoning

Here is an example of logical reasoning: The mother goes to the grocery store that afternoon and sees her son's friend, Scott, along with his parents. She mentions that she was sorry that her son did not get to go to the pool with their family this afternoon, but she thanks them for the invitation. At that point, Scott's mother says that they had no plans to go to the pool that day and that there had been no invitation extended, although that plan sounds fun and they should do it in the future. At this point, Max's mother draws a logical inference that her son had lied to her earlier so that he could text a message to someone. Why else would Max have made up the story about swimming with Scott? The mother rejects the idea that Max wanted to go swimming and rejects the idea that her son was truthful with her.

- Draw inferences or conclusions that are justified by the evidence.
- Logically infer a new statement from those statements or beliefs you already think are true.
- Reject new or old beliefs that are not justified and that do not fit with other things you know to be true.

6. Weighing the Pros and Cons

An example of weighing the pros and cons occurs when Max's mother envisions what might occur when she confronts Max about his lies. She reasons, "If I act as if I do not know about the lie, I cannot have a conversation with Max about the importance of honesty. If I go home angry and yell at Max, he is likely to hide in his room and ignore me. If I can control my anger but let him know the severity of his offense and then discipline him in a level-headed way, he is more likely to understand that I value honesty, obedience, fairness, and our relationship." She decides on the last option and intends, as part of his disciplinary repercussions, to have him write a two-page paper on the value of honesty.

- Envision the potential good and bad consequences of a decision. Carefully consider the likelihood of the consequences and the severity of their impact. Then make a decision based on all the aspects you have considered.

7. Transforming Knowledge

Here is an example of transforming knowledge: As the mom gets home from the store, she walks into the living room and finds that Max has been crying. She decides to investigate what he was feeling instead of telling him of the new information she had found out from Scott's parents and the new consequences he had earned. While engaging with him in conversation, she realizes that Max is upset because he had found out that his girlfriend, Dina, was in a very serious car wreck and was being airlifted to a hospital in a larger city. The earlier text that he sent had not been to Scott but had been to Dina's parents. He was too ashamed to tell her about it earlier because he was afraid that he would cry. That's why he made up the lie about needing to tell Scott's parents that he couldn't swim that afternoon; he needed to get information about Dina.

Max's mom knows how to administer proper discipline and how to be fair. She had planned fair discipline for a son who had been repeatedly disobedient. She had been fair to add additional punishment for his dishonesty. However, the most recent information about Dina shed some light on the entire situation. Max's mom realizes that she must transform the original plans to discipline her son with limits on texting and with writing a paper on honesty, and instead, make this teaching situation more about being open about our feelings and about the acceptance of difficult truths. She begins to help her son gather information about the accident and Dina's condition, showing him that gathering proper information can help people deal with fear. At a later time, when their emotions were not so fragile, they could discuss the importance of honesty, even in a difficult situation.

- Understand the condition, nature, form, or function of a procedure, concept, or process, and alter it to fit another context.
- Use existing knowledge innovatively to produce something new.

8. Being Clear and Precise

An example of clarity and precision would occur if Max's mother articulated what a lie is and how (or whether) it differs from "partial truths."

- Being able to express what one means to say in words that reflect no more and no less than they intend.
- Understanding a concept, plan, or procedure and being able to articulate what it is and is not.
- Using language so that other people grasp the intended meaning without misunderstanding.

People use these skills in a wide variety of situations, not just about concepts like fairness. They affect practical life. Further, some of these skills overlap and, in some circumstances, some are more relevant to the situation than others.

Consider another example. James, who is trying to determine if he should have surgery on his back, needs to utilize these skills. For the sake of brevity, we will consider the first two—analyzing and judging with objective standards.

Analyzing involves breaking down information into smaller parts to discover its nature, functionality, and relationships. It also requires us to think of the ramifications of the view or action and to identify the assumptions inherent in the view. Without thinking critically, someone might notice that he has back pain and recognize that a surgeon would suggest back surgery. He might plan to have back surgery without giving it another thought. The critical thinker, on the other hand, would analyze the situation so he could make the best decision.

Suppose James is a critical thinker. What will he analyze?

James could analyze various aspects of his situation and his health problem. Let's consider the back problem first. Instead of noticing that he is in constant pain in his back and knowing that one surgeon suggested that he have surgery, James must break down the issue by questioning:

- whether the surgery is likely to fix a back issue like his;
- whether the quality of life that he currently has with his back pain is worth the risk that is involved in back surgery;
- his past experiences with surgeries and his likelihood of healing;
- whether he has underlying health problems like diabetes or other risk factors that could complicate the surgery;
- the effects anesthesia might have on him for months to come;
- whether another specialist at another health management institution would also suggest that he have surgery at this point; if there are alternatives, pain management or physical therapy, that might help without surgery;
- whether the surgeon is inclined to suggest surgery rather than something else because he is financially motivated to perform a surgery.

He could also analyze, by breaking apart concepts and considering the ramifications of the surgery, different aspects of his situation that are not directly health-related. For instance:

- Considering the amount of savings he has right now and the time off that he has accrued from work, is it economically feasible for him to get the surgery right now?
- Will he have assistance around the house when he is discharged from the hospital after the surgery? If not, he may need to wait to find someone who can help him before he schedules the surgery.
- Does the expense of his daughter's upcoming wedding affect the availability of extra funds he might need to pay for what insurance won't pay?

Economic, social, psychological, and health reasons all factor into James's decision. The critical thinker will try to consider each option as he deliberates about what choice to make.

Before reading further, ask yourself:

- How might James judge the situation using standards?
- What standards might apply to this situation?

Pause here and try to provide an answer.

One way that James could **judge using standards** is for him to create a list of physical outcomes that he would expect if the surgery were successful. Would he need to be out of pain completely, or just most of the time? Would he need to be able to bend down to put his shoes on his feet without assistance, or is being out of pain enough? Would it be good enough for the pain to not be in his back, but for him to still have trouble with occasional pain shooting down his legs? These expectations are standards and can be listed in clear, declarative sentences (i.e., statement, or "propositions") that are either true or false. They are rules by which he can judge the expected success of the operation. (There are other standards that he may apply as well, such as the reputation of the surgeon, but we will limit this discussion to his physical expectations.)

Notice that different people may answer the questions differently. To risk having surgery, some people may judge they would need to be completely pain-free. Others may think that it would be good enough to have any pain less than they have now. The way they answer these questions are personal to them. The fact that they hold these standards, no matter how they answer the question, also suggests that they have taken personal ownership of the standards. This is similar to how we form some beliefs. When we believe something, we take ownership of that belief. It becomes ours. It is personal.

1.3.2 Subjectivity, Objectivity, and Personal Standards

There is an important distinction that should be made now. This is the distinction between subjective and objective. Just because something is personal, this does not mean that it is not true. Similarly, just because something is personal, this does not mean that it *is* true. What makes something true? Truth is connected to an objective reality in the right way.

Objectivity is connected with a Reality that exists outside of the mental life of a person. For example, it will be objectively true that a guitar is propped up in the corner of my room if there is a guitar propped up in the corner of my room. If I am unaware of the guitar, this does not make the guitar disappear. If I'm hallucinating and think that the guitar is a person, this does not transform the guitar into a person. It is common sense and grounded in the principles of logic to say that a guitar is not a person but that it is a guitar. My desire that it be in another room or that it be a person does not change the fact that it is a guitar sitting in a particular room in the corner. Reality acts as a standard or rule that is objective. Our minds should try to adapt to what is. We should make our beliefs reflect what is real. If we get an answer wrong, this means that we need to better conform to the standard of Reality. If we get an answer right, then it accurately reflects Reality. You may notice that "reality" is capitalized sometimes. Some philosophers capitalize it when referencing an objectively-true, mind-independent Reality. They will use a lowercase "r" to refer to a perception someone has of what is real, or to things that are subjectively, but not objectively, true.

> **Objective:** Separate from a person's desires, beliefs, and biases. It is based in Reality and Truth, apart from a person's perception of it.
>
> **Subjective:** Dependent on a person's desires, beliefs, and biases.
>
> **Personal standards:** Standards that we believe to be true and may be more or less objective, depending on the nature of the topic and our criteria for accepting the belief.
>
> Note that a critical thinker tries to be objective in most situations unless the topic (like a preference for one ice cream over another) is purely subjective.

Subjectivity is dependent upon the mental life and processes of the individual person. It is not connected to Reality in the same way that objectivity is. If I prefer roller skating to swimming as a hobby, there needs to be no further connection to reality than the fact "I do like roller skating better than swimming." There is no objective standard that roller skating is better than swimming. No feature of reality makes roller skating better than swimming. This is subjective because it is a preference that is based purely on my desire. If I decide in the future that swimming is more fun than roller skating, I am not wrong to change my mind.

What does this have to do with James and the decision he must make about whether or not to have surgery on his back? For one thing, while James may personally hold the questions about the success of the surgery as a standard by which to judge whether or not he should have the surgery, these standards are not merely subjective. Put differently, James may hold personal standards of expectation, but these standards cannot merely be *subjective* standards that are not connected to Reality. It would make no sense for James to expect that he be able to be a great skydiver merely because he has surgery. Acquiring the skills to become a great skydiver is not closely connected to back surgery, so it would make no sense to judge the surgery's success on an irrelevant and unrealistic standard. One does not become a skydiver by having surgery. There is a connection, however, between James having back surgery and being able to twist, bend over, get up from a seated position, and have less pain. These are relevant standards that, in some way, connect what James can subjectively expect with what is Real and possible. Since James' expectations and physical condition are highly relevant to him becoming a skydiver, some people may be tempted to think his expectations—what is in James' mind (i.e., his "reality")—is all that matters. Certainly, his perception of himself and his expectations are very important. However, these only have power when they are connected to the Reality outside of his mind. His conception of reality must cohere with what's actually true in order for his expectations to materialize. Without this connection of his subjective reality to objective Reality, James is only delusional or, at best, wrongly optimistic. Standards for judging cannot merely be dependent on unrealistic subjective desires. James may wish to become a skydiver eventually, and he can even ask the doctor if that activity would be advisable for him to work toward after his surgery. But the standard for judging whether or not to have the surgery has to be connected to some real possibility that is outside of his preference, desires, or hopes if it is to be meaningful and useful. In this case, it has to be connected to something that the doctor can closely correlate with similar surgeries and that can be observable.

What does this teach us about critical thinkers? The standards that critical thinkers use to make good judgments are not merely subjective standards. In other words, a good critical thinker will not be "critical" or "judgy." Part of the value of critical thinking is that it allows us to understand the viewpoints of others, even if we don't agree with them. It allows us to respect other people by listening to them and respectfully presenting information. If a one cannot distinguish between his preferences and those things that are objectively true, this person is likely to be unable to value other people's beliefs and viewpoints. Further, he will spend too much mental energy evaluating things that do not matter. He will condemn a mixture of things—some of which will not deserve to be condemned—and will not always be accurate. People will lose value in his perspective and he will miss the opportunity to tell them to share the things which are true. He will also be more close-minded, which will hinder his ability to gather information and it will put a barrier between him and other people.

Overall, there is nothing wrong with judging, if we judge the right things, with the right criteria, in the right way, and with the right attitude. We must judge things, people, events, prices, advertisements, and situations regularly. But judging can go wrong when people try to enforce their subjective opinions on others as if those standards were objectively true. The critical thinker will not condemn someone else for preferring chocolate-covered raspberries rather than chocolate-covered cherries. A person may have a personal preference, but

> Part of the value of critical thinking is that it allows us to understand the viewpoints of others, even if we don't agree with them.

there is no objective rule that cherries are better than raspberries when covered with chocolate. A person is free to like what he or she wants to like when the matter is merely subjective. Thus, the critical thinker will not judge other people for not holding the same preferences or opinions as him about things that have no standard other than the person's preference. This is because critical thinkers try to be unbiased. Being unbiased, however, does not mean that critical thinkers lack personal convictions or that they accept everything as true. People can rightfully and personally hold some standards that can still be used to judge others' behaviors and views. But for personally held standards to be logically convincing to others or to have substance to them, they have to be connected to Reality or Truth in some way. They must possess a degree of objectivity.

Objectivity's connection to Reality or Truth makes it more public than a privately held preference. You can converse with others about objective standards in a meaningful way and apply the standards in a larger context than you could if you merely applied your personal preferences. For example, consider the difference between these two statements about a standard:

The law says that I can't drive over 65 on this highway.
versus
I tell my cat-loving friend that dogs are better than cats.

The speed limit standard is objective and refers to a clear way of judging that all people must try to uphold. Going 66 or anything over that is technically considered speeding. The second claim, however, is a personal preference and, although there is some information that my friend gains about me when she sees that I prefer dogs, there is no objective Truth being conveyed to her that will make her get rid of her cat and adopt a dog. My preference, in itself, has no right to influence her preference.

Sometimes people are mistaken about a standard. I could think that the speed limit is 45 on a particular stretch of the highway, but a knowledgeable friend may tell me that it was raised to 55 recently. I could mistakenly think that a bronze medal in the Olympics is the same as a gold medal, but pretty much everyone would tell me that first place is gold and that the metal is not the same as the bronze. This is one reason that a person's subjective views do not create what's objectively true. When people disagree, they should look for an objective standard by which to judge each of their views. The view that is most closely reflecting Reality, or what is true, should be the view that remains. The mistaken view should be rejected.

If you have adopted the right standards, most reasonable people will accept the standard if they are thinking logically and have enough information. Sometimes in legal studies, reference is made to the "reasonable person" standard. While there are always people who are cantankerous, misinformed, illogical, or purely rebellious and will not agree, the rational person will come to many of the same conclusions as other rational people because we share rationality (i.e., the ability to reason). If there is a guitar sitting in the corner of my room, then most people will agree that there is a guitar sitting in the corner of my room. If part of being a parent means that you do not neglect your kids' well-being, then most people will agree that neglect should be avoided. If getting back surgery is not likely to help my pain or improve my mobility and it is a risky surgery, most people will not advise that I get the surgery. In other words, the "reasonable person" will agree with the other "reasonable people."

Let's think back to James again. To make a good decision, he would also need to **gather, assess, and use information wisely.** This would include getting background information on the surgeon and hospital, their success rate, and the recovery rate of people in circumstances similar to his. He would be utilizing information well if he also talked to people who had a similar surgery and got their experiences. He may also want to get information about alternative forms of treatment that may help him instead of surgery. He would assess the credibility of the studies done on similar back surgeries and judge whether the sources that provide this information are unfairly biased. James would use **logical reasoning** if he puts aside the fear he has of all surgeries to decide whether to have the surgery based on factual evidence. He would **weigh the pros and cons** if he considers the good and bad points of each one of his options.

Apply 1.3a

1. Think of a time when you used the above skills. (i.e., Analyzing; Judging with objective standards; Discriminating; Gathering, assessing, and using information wisely; Logical reasoning; Weighing the pros and cons; Transforming knowledge; Being clear and precise). For each skill, define it. Then, explain the context in which you used the skills. If it is not obvious, tell how your actions were an example of this skill.

2. Which of the eight critical thinking skills is operative in the following scenario: Laney works in a women's care clinic that sees at least twenty-five patients each morning. The policies suggest that if a man is providing care to the women that day, then there must be at least one woman working there who is available to see patients with him. One day, Laney was the only woman to come to work that day. She had twenty-five patients to record information about and to see with the male provider. Of course, she couldn't take the patients in turn because this would prolong their wait time and make everyone very unhappy. She also knew that she could not leave the male provider alone to do an exam on a patient because it would possibly make the patients feel uncomfortable and it would break company policy. Laney decided to get information on two patients, one after the other, while the doctor talked to one patient in more depth. Then, she would come back to the provider before he began any physical examination or treatments. She also asked the receptionist at the front desk to cheerfully reassure the patients in the waiting room that they would be seen as soon as possible.

Apply 1.3b

Explain how one or more of the eight critical thinking skills mentioned above are operative in the following situations.

1. "The first way that you played that piano song was better than the second because your use of dynamics and phrasing was lost in the second one."

2. "I used to feel bad because I was smaller than everyone else my age. It made me ashamed of myself. But now I realize that people come in all different shapes and sizes. This realization made me no longer feel bad about my size."

3. "These pills that my grandmother takes are both very small and white. They have letters inscribed on each pill, but she cannot see the letters well enough. I have sorted them out for her because she had them accidentally mixed."

4. "I did not know if I should drink the water in this stream, but I drank it. I did not have any capsules that kill germs to add to my bottle and there was a sign that said the water was not safe to consume without treatment. However, I was very thirsty and dehydrated. I was not going to be able to get to a clean water source anytime soon."

1.4 Foundational Principles

Now that you're familiar with some of the skills that you will use as a critical thinker, you will be introduced to three principles that undergird clear and logical thinking. You will also distinguish among facts, reasoned judgments, and opinions before this chapter concludes.

Logic is the branch of philosophy that studies reasoning. Reasoning occurs when we encounter information and then draw conclusions from it. Logic makes prescriptions about what makes sense to think and conclude. In other words, it is the art or science of reasoning well. Logic guides people in *how* to think but not necessarily *what* to think. It gives general principles or rules for helping us understand Reality and what is true. These principles have to be applied skillfully to the various situations and pieces of information that we encounter.

Like almost any other subject, there must be a foundation upon which to build our knowledge. Since ancient times, logic has been built on three main rules, commonly called laws. These rules are features of reality that are presumably inescapable. To use an analogy, think about how human beings must breathe air to live. This is how our body works and this principle holds because of the nature of human beings. Analogously, the following rules of logic hold because of the nature of Reality. Someone could deny that humans must breathe air, but one's life will not operate well (and soon, not at all) if one does not breathe it. Similarly, a someone can deny that humans have to follow the logical laws, but their life will not operate well (and in some cases, some important life occurrances can't happen at all) if one does not use them.

1.4.1 The Law of Excluded Middle

The law of excluded middle is the principle that a statement cannot be something between true and false. No concept falls in between truth and falsity. For instance, I can say For example, the statement "All violins have four strings" is either true or false. Someone may point out that some violins may have a broken string and only have three, or one may have been altered in an abnormal way to include an extra string. When exceptions are noted, then the first statement can be considered false or can be revised to accommodate the abnormal circumstances so that it can then become a true statement. For instance, I could qualify the original

nothing can be between true and false

statement to make it more specific and thus, more clearly true by saying "It is standard that all traditional violins that have not been altered and are in tact have four strings." This qualified statement is true, whereas (if one is being excessively picky) the first statement about violins could be construed as false. But meaning of the the statement itself is either true or false. There is nothing in between truth and falsity if our topic is specific and narrow enough.

You may be thinking that a statement can be possibly true or possibly false. There are certainly many cases where "possibly" or "maybe" is the proper answer. If maybe is the answer, this just means that the truth is waiting to occur in the future. Many things are dependent upon other things. The girl that asks her parents if she can go out with her friends this weekend may be answered that they will have to "wait and see how her final exam grades are." This does not break the law of excluded middle. This just indicates that we must be very particular about the truth that we are trying to capture. If we say, "Linae's social life is dependent on her earning a good exam grade," this statement is true even though we do not know what the future holds for the grade or her social life. The statement, nevertheless, reflects something true at this point. After Linae earns an A on her exam, then the future would reflect a different scenario and set of events. Then, we could answer whether or not Linae was able to hang out with her friends. But again, she either gets to hang out with them or she does not. Even if she gets to hang out with them, but has to leave unexpectedly after five minutes, she still got to hang out with them.

1.4.2 The Law of Identity

The law of identity is the principle that something is what it is; it is not something other than what it is. This is a basic and foundational law. It is so fundamental to our thinking that most of us never assume differently—and we are correct! In the moment when we are speaking of a thing, for example, things are as they are. Further, certain essences can't ever be different from what they are. I know my car no matter what parking lot I have parked in because my car is my car. It is the car that it is and it has the specific characteristics that it has, and this enables me to identify my car from another that is similar. If something exists, it exists with a particular identity. A thing is what it is, and it is not what it is not. For instance, a flower is a flower, and it is not a light bulb, a hippopotamus, or a snowstorm. It is a flower. Of course, people know how to use something for various purposes, and situations may change. A flower could be used as a corsage or as a symbol of affection. It could be used as a bookmark if it is dried, or to fragrance a room. A flower could be used as a grave marker or to celebrate the birth of a new baby. Despite its uses and the way that we may reappropriate it, a flower is a flower. I may sell my car and it no longer be MY car, but it is still the particular car that it is. Similarly, a "1" is a "1." It is not a 2 or any other number. The letter Q is the letter Q and is not any other letter, nor is it a number or a flower. Accordingly, a true statement, based on the law of identity, is a true statement. Truth is truth and it does not vary from person to person based on different perspectives or preferences. The law of identity is important for several reasons but the main one is that it makes things knowable. It makes our world easier to navigate, as well. I know which car to get into in the parking lot because my car is the car that it is.

[handwritten margin note: an item is what it is, cannot be another item but can be used in different ways]

1.4.3 The Law of Noncontradiction

The last logical law will be most referenced in this book. It is **the law of noncontradiction**. The law of noncontradiction states that a proposition cannot be both true and false. Don't confuse this with the law of excluded middle. The law of excluded middle eliminates the possibility that there's something other than true or false when referring to a statement. The law of noncontradiction shows that a proposition and its opposite cannot both be true at the same time in the same way. "A" cannot equal "not-A." I cannot accurately state that an ear of corn is not an ear of corn and be saying something true with each statement. Perhaps I could if I was speaking figuratively about an ear of corn or using it in an illusion or magic trick. But if I am using language in the normal way and saying "I'm holding an ear of corn in my hand," then I cannot at the same time also truthfully claim "I'm not holding an ear of corn in my hand." Of course,

[handwritten margin note: nothing can be true and false]

Second, you need to know how the agents interact. Sometimes the parts of the complex system are connected really tightly together, and the patterns are pretty predictable. Sometimes the parts are loosely connected—sometimes even disconnected—so you cannot predict or control how they will act individually. And, you have no idea what kinds of patterns they might generate together. If you want to manage the collaborative CAS, you can add or remove, strengthen or weaken the connections among the parts of the system. The more connected they are, the easier it will be to predict and control. But the less freedom individual agents will have to use their strengths. I have been teaching face-to-face for almost four decades and love the emotional energy shared in workshops, discussions, etc. Four years ago I began teaching online courses and had to find my online voice as I missed the live interactions between myself and students. I changed my writing style to be more conversational and less academic. This seemed to help somewhat, but online exchanges remain different than being physically together. We collaborate differently as teachers, learners, and leaders.

The third way to influence a CAS is to name and frame the patterns as they emerge. When you name a pattern (trust, performance, health, and so on), it makes it concrete and accessible for people. You help a group come to terms with their situation. A name for a pattern helps people share stories, build routines and rituals, and come to shared understanding. The way you name a pattern is an important leadership challenge in any collaborative effort. Some names restrict options for action and others expand the options.

For example, when a team is not interacting and people are reluctant to take even small risks by speaking, you might name the pattern "lack of trust." That may be true, but it isn't very useful. If the problem is lack of trust, all you can do is to encourage people to trust each other more, and we all know how little that works.

On the other hand, if you name the issue differently—difficulty listening or being heard, not following through on commitments, talking about people and not to them—then you have lots of options for action.

How you name the pattern helps you manage in CAS, even when you are not in control.

Challenges of Collaboration

In the best of all possible worlds, collaboration creates a whole that is greater than the sum of the parts. People bring their unique skills and identities, interact in respectful and curious ways, and plan and take aligned action for themselves and the collective. On the other hand, few of us live in this best of all possible worlds. Many different factors challenge effective collaboration.

Conflicting agendas lead people to hoard information or dominate processes, so that the power of diversity is lost in the struggle for control. The purpose of collaborative action is to harvest the divergent strengths and objectives of diverse groups. When differences are too great, or they are not discussed openly, then dialogue breaks down and conflict often follows.

Unclear goals and objectives draw in resources and hopes, but do not deliver on the promise of shared action. Collaborations often begin with great hopes and idealistic opportunities. Over time, as hope turns to action and ideals to reality, the outcomes and impacts of collaborations frequently fall short of predictions.

Constrained resources cause people to over-control and hold back resources of the part, even when they might be better used by the whole. When funding is allocated to existing silos, both within and between organizations, it is challenging to access funding to support collaborative work.

Prejudice and bias keep people and groups from interacting freely and openly. This is not just cultural, gender, or racial bias. Those are certainly barriers to effective collaboration. Others include professional and non-professional; wealthy and impoverished; urban and rural; union and management; clinical specialties; and academic pedigrees.

All of these challenges are true, but we believe one challenge surpasses all of these. Professionals have been trained to be experts in their own right, not as players on a collaborative team. Effective collaboration requires a very specific set of skills that are seldom taught and often overlooked. Many of those skills relate directly to what you learned in Module 1: Lead at the Edge of Uncertainty about emerging patterns in Complex Adaptive Systems.

Successful collaborations exhibit patterns of open dialogue, respect, and empathy. The same keys for leading in complexity will serve well in collaboration. They are summarized in the following table.

Lead in Complexity	Collaborative Patterns	Path Toward Effective Collaboration
Complex Adaptive System	Agents come together in collaborative action, interact with each other virtually or face-to-face, and patterns emerge from their interactions. After the patterns begin to form, they sustain by influencing action of agents in the future.	Make sure the right people are at the table. Acknowledge and leverage difference. Facilitate effective dialogue—speaking and listening. Name and reinforce positive patterns as they emerge.
Adaptive Action	Observe WHAT are current patterns. Consider SO WHAT are tensions and options for change. Take action with NOW WHAT to make a difference in the emergent pattern.	Engage all players in Adaptive Action. Encourage Adaptive Action of part, whole, and greater whole. Don't get stuck in any of the steps. Iterate, iterate, iterate.

Table 5: Collaboration and Adaptive Action

When you use your leadership intelligence to set conditions, then the collaborative patterns of trust and productivity are more likely to appear. Even if they do not show up right away, you can continue your Adaptive Actions, finding new approaches until one makes a difference to the whole.

Circle of Control

In the *Seven Habits of Highly Effective People* (Covey, 2013), Stephen Covey talks about one of the major challenges in leading collaborative efforts. It is about the differences between span of control, span of influence, and span of concern.

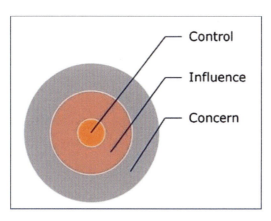

Figure 5: Circle of Control

41

As a leader, you know the range of work that you control. These are the parts of your work where the Complex Adaptive System is tightly constrained. Strong similarities, few differences, and tight connections keep the patterns under control. Some things lie outside that range of control, but you still have influence to affect those patterns by either formal or informal means. Beyond that, there are issues and questions that you have no influence over, but you have concern about them.

In complex situations, your circles of influence and control shrink, and your circle of concern gets larger. We often find ourselves talking about and focusing on the world of concern where we are helpless and victimized. Your responsibility as a leader is to counteract this tendency. You and your team should focus your attention on the things you control and have influence over. As you do, those circles will expand, and the circle of helpless concern will begin to shrink.

The challenge is magnified in collaborative relationships. As the system gets larger and more diverse, as more people have influence and exercise their control, you can begin to feel out of control. You may even feel that you are being victimized by your collaborative partners. This is a very unproductive game to play, and there is a sure-fire exit from it: Adaptive Action.

If you find yourself in this situation, ask yourself:

▶ What are the things I can control in this collaboration? What can I influence?

▶ So what am I doing now to make a difference where I can? So what might I do differently?

▶ Now what will I do to shift the pattern and improve the productivity of this collaborative relationship?

One Sticky Issue of Collaboration

In this Module, we will ask you to focus on a specific Sticky Issue about collaboration or negotiation that is affecting you right now. As you learn new skills and approaches during this Module, we will invite you to use them in your own real-time Adaptive Action to make a difference in the patterns of your leadership, learning, and teaching.

Three Ways to Bring People Together

We have a variety of models and methods that we use to help make your Adaptive Action easier and more powerful. In this section, we will share three models that we have used to great effect when we are working with bringing people together into shared action. They include:

▶ Radical Inquiry
▶ Simple Rules
▶ STAR

Radical Inquiry

Radical Inquiry is a way to structure a conversation—either a reflection for yourself, a conversation with a small group, or a dialogue in a large convening. The purpose is to discover the pattern that is shared across the whole group, without asking any individual to risk or sacrifice their own identity in the process. The questions are open-ended. There are no "right" or "wrong" answers. The purpose of the dialogue is to come to an "excellent enough" consensus about what the work of the collaboration is or will be. The questions match Adaptive Action and our definition of patterns, so Radical Inquiry is a way of weaving HSD into a gathering without making a big deal out of it. (For more information, refer to Appendix 3.)

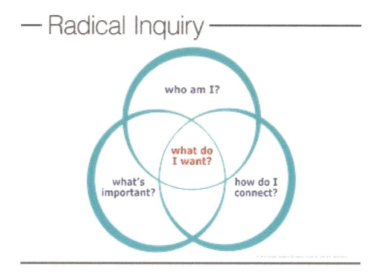

Figure 6: Radical Inquiry

> ***Radical Inquiry:*** *Question to help an individual or group find the pattern that grounds them in identity and action.*

The questions can be about one person or about many. As you work in collaborative settings, you will probably find the group version most helpful.

Who are we together to do this work? This question can be surprisingly deep and meaningful. Working once with a team of prevention specialists, their answers to this question ranged from:

- ▶ We are protectors of public health
- ▶ We are teachers and trainers for the public good
- ▶ We are health professionals working in the community

Each of these answers brought up a very different picture of their work together. No wonder they had experienced difficulty working together in the past. As we talked, they came to a shared understanding: We are public health resources for the communities we serve. While this might not be a perfect statement, it was good enough for the group to move forward together. It was "excellent enough."

As we do this work, what is most important to us? This question can reach into values, or it can be measures of assessment or resources, or beliefs about the work. As a group discusses the differences they have about what's important, patterns begin to appear that tell you a great deal about what the group is and what they will be able to accomplish together. My public health group brainstormed and wrote many ideas about what was important on sticky notes. We then sorted the notes into clusters, from which they decided the following things were important to them in their work:

▶ Knowing our communities—how they are alike and how they are different
▶ Equity of health outcomes across the communities
▶ Supporting health and wellbeing for all—including us!

All of the brainstormed items fell into one or another of these categories, so the group felt comfortable with the list. They also had the opportunity to talk about differences that make a difference at many levels—individuals, communities, the team, and citizens. They want patterns that work across the whole, part, and greater whole.

How do we connect to be most productive and effective? This question, of course, is about the connections that hold the CAS together. Sometimes groups will talk about methods and media for connection, such as email, meetings, teleconferences. This group, however, chose to talk about the ways they communicate. This is what they came up with:

▶ We speak our truths
▶ We listen to each other
▶ We co-create the future

From this short description, I'm sure you can see how this group came together in their collaborative efforts. You can also imagine how bumpy their work would be if they had not found ways to talk together about the patterns that inform their work.

No two groups will answer these questions in the same way, and over time, a group's answers might change. Imagine how this group of public health professionals might see themselves differently in a time of a natural disaster.

▶ Who are we? Sources of information
▶ What is important to us? Speed and accuracy
▶ How do we connect? Connecting people to resources

This is quite a different pattern, but one that is fit for function for a very different complex environment.

I was a small-group facilitator, a tutor, in problem-based learning at the University of New Mexico School of Medicine. Groups of students usually stayed together for six to eight weeks depending on the Module of study. The first meeting of a new group of first year medical students always felt to me like opening a present, filled with curiosity and interest in learning. We'd take some time to introduce ourselves, talk about why we were here, how we got here, our aspirations, how we liked to learn and work together.

What was important in the beginning of a new group was that everyone participate, that we would help each other do the work of learning, that we would be respectful of others and respectful of the time we had together.

We talked about connecting through sharing what we found pursuing various questions that arose in our work. Speaking and listening well with each other was a key quality for learning. Regular high quality group and individual reflections and feedback set conditions for short-term improvement. We agreed to self, peer, and group assess at each meeting. What did the group feel went well today? What could we each change next time we meet to contribute to our inquiry and learning?

Simple Rules

Simple Rules help diverse individuals make decisions for themselves and still create a systemic pattern. Based on studies of natural flocks of birds and schools of fish, Simple Rules assume that if everyone follows the same rules, regardless of their circumstances, then the whole will generate coherent patterns like a Complex Adaptive System.

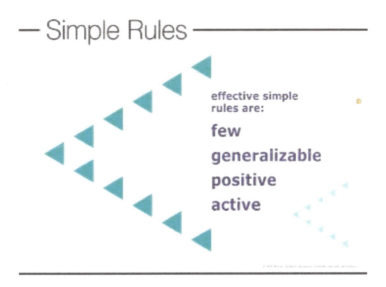

Figure 7: Simple Rules

You have already encountered the Human Systems Dynamics Institute Simple Rules. We have been using them to evaluate the patterns that emerge from our time together. Many other groups have different Simple Rules to shape their cultures.

- ▶ In many cultures: Honor ancestors
- ▶ In governance: Balance freedom and equality
- ▶ One of my clients: Assume positive intent
- ▶ In my family: Bring a solution with every complaint

In all of these cases everyone in the group is expected to follow the rules. It might look different, depending on your role, power, or resources. Still, wherever you are, when you follow the rules, you fit into the flock.

One hospital I am aware of has a simple rule: Welcome everyone. I was amazed at the patterns of warmth and delight I felt when I entered, even before I knew their rule.

Not all rules are Simple Rules. Here are the rules for Simple Rules:

- ▶ Begin with a verb—they tell you what to do, not what to think or say
- ▶ Include 7 or fewer—because you want to be able to remember them quickly and easily
- ▶ Pertain to everyone in the group, all the time—so that the patterns are consistent and coherent
- ▶ Review and revise them as circumstances change
- ▶ Include rules that set conditions for the patterns as in the Radical Inquiry

You can use the Simple Rules in two ways. First, you can look at the pattern you observe, and try to figure out what implicit rules were at work to create that pattern in the past. Or, you can consider the patterns you want to create, and generate a set of rules that will support behaviors that are likely to generate those patterns in the future.

Either way, it is best if you can engage the group in finding their own Simple Rules. Not only are they likely to be more realistic and useful, but they will also already be accepted by the group, so implementation will be a breeze.

We asked teachers planning an innovation for a medical school what basic rules would inform all aspects of the new curriculum. After several discussions among many different groups of teachers in different departments, they decided:

► Teach and learn—everybody, all the time
► Use real settings and with real stories
► Assume responsibility for your learning, as individuals and as groups
► Focus on clinical experience, early and in a sustainable way
► Integrate the sciences basic to medicine throughout the curriculum
► Ask questions at the frontier of your understanding
► Stay immersed in the community

These rules were applied explicitly during the design and faculty development phases of the curriculum and implicitly during implementation.

STAR

In the early 1990s, Brenda Zimmerman, a friend and colleague in Canada, was working with boards of directors of non-profit organizations, helping them work together creatively. She realized that what they wanted and needed were Generative Teams—ones for which the whole was greater than the sum of the parts. Not all teams have to be generative. Sometimes you want a team to do exactly what is expected with reliability and rigor, but sometimes you need your team to create something new together. That is a Generative Team because it generates new energy and ideas as it does its work. (For more information, refer to Appendix 3.)

Brenda was one of the pioneers in using complexity to support leaders and teams, so she turned to her understanding of Complex Adaptive Systems and, what we now refer to as the conditions for self-organizing, to see how to set conditions for generative action. The result was the STAR Model. (also see Appendix 3).

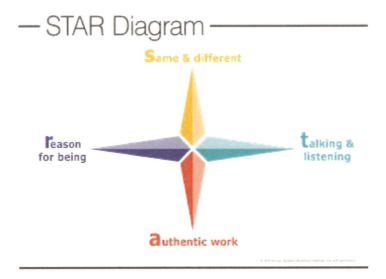

Figure 8: STAR Diagram

> **STAR:** *Set conditions for a group—team or community—to work generatively together to co-create something that they could not do by themselves.*

The STAR focuses on four characteristics that set conditions for generative relationships. These features influence the emergent patterns of the group, so they shift emergent patterns.

▶ **Same and Different**—Coherent, generative groups need enough similarity to hold them together and enough difference to create patterns and tension for energy and change.

▶ **Talking and Listening**—When people come together to accomplish a task, whether in the short term or across time, it's critical that each person is allowed to contribute and that each person listens to the contributions of others.

▶ **Authentic Work**—Teams need to do "real" work together. The challenges they face, the products they create, the opportunities they explore—all must be of real value to each of them and to the larger system of which they are a part.

▶ **Reason for Being**—Groups need a compelling reason for working together, both in short-term, periodic meetings, and in longer term of their overall purpose.

You can use the STAR in any part of the Adaptive Action cycle to answer the questions:

▶ **What?** See the current patterns of a group
▶ **So What?** Understand why it is, or is not, working in generative ways
▶ **Now What?** Choose interventions that will improve the generativity of the group

As a leader, you can use the STAR in many different ways. For example, use it to:

▶ Set conditions—including expectations, relationships, and ground rules—for a team to be productive
▶ Establish a context for shared leadership roles
▶ Work with stakeholders
▶ Support interdisciplinary teams and practices
▶ Focus on issues of culture and productivity in groups
▶ Plan and structure meetings

The STAR is a useful tool for teaching, as well, especially in practice-based settings. You can use it to:

▶ Coach and mentor teams of learners
▶ Design effective inquiry-based experiences
▶ Collaborate with other faculty members
▶ Integrate teaching and research
▶ Manage your relationships with individual learners
▶ Work with others to integrate learning and care delivery

The STAR framework supports reflection and organization of formative and summative evaluation of a medical education curriculum innovation. For example, the parallel curriculum tracts at the University of New Mexico collected short-term, mid- and long-term data about curriculum context, experience, learning, impact on the school, teachers, students, university and the State. These are complex, and patterns are the best way to look at them over time and across different learning sites. Short cycles of Adaptive Action at the local level were useful for leaders and participants of the innovation and helped them to make small useful corrections along the way. Over time the collection of small changes emerged as patterns of the whole and greater whole that informed the program, the institution, and the field of medical education. The evaluation followed the participants in the parallel tracks for fifteen years after which time it became an institutionalized component of the medical school. Today, it is one of the few longitudinal curriculum evaluations in the United States. The Simple Rules and the STAR framework guided leadership, teachers and researchers and helped them to sustain and keep learning.

One of the optional resources for this Module includes an assessment you can use for yourself or with a group to explore the generative nature of a particular team or group. Please complete the STAR Assessment now for your Sticky Issue, and reflect on and respond to the following questions.

2.2 Patterns in Your Sticky Issue

Reflect on these questions and share your thoughts online (less than 25 words):

► **What patterns do you see in your collaboration Sticky Issue when you consider any one of the tools you learned in this Module so far:**
  ▷ **Complex Adaptive System (CAS)**
  ▷ **Circles of Control**
  ▷ **Radical Inquiry?**
  ▷ **Simple Rules?**
  ▷ **The STAR?**
► **So what are the patterns you are seeing in the team as a result of your current conditions?**
► **Now what can you do to strengthen your team and leverage the strengths of the team to become more generative?**

Troubleshooting to Get Back on Track

Collaborations do not always work smoothly. Teams get into conflict; cooperative agreements stall; inter-professional practice teams get frustrated and give up. You can set conditions for success, but over time, issues arise, patterns shift, and you need to take Adaptive Action.

In this section, we will look at a way to use Adaptive Action to see, understand, and influence patterns when collaborations break down.

Conflict in Collaboration

When there are too many differences in a group, it is natural to want to protect your organization, your interests and yourself from harm, stress, and danger. If you view conflict as a battle, an attack, or a threat, you can get caught up in an emotionally charged "action – reaction" cycle that leads to a lose-lose situation. Instead, consider conflict as an open engagement in which the goal is to keep playing, keep the conversation going, and create optimal conditions for both sides to succeed.

In human systems dynamics, we think about conflict as tension. Individuals or groups are different, so tension develops between them. That tension is not necessarily bad because it can lead to learning, growth, and change. The tension of conflict can be destructive though, if there is no way to release it productively through dialogue or shared action. Effective collaboration provides both—dialogue and shared action. It requires joint Adaptive Action that focuses on the interests, not on the positions, taken by both sides. The goal of collaboration is to replace the tensions of conflict with a new pattern that satisfies the interests of both sides efficiently, and does that without bitterness or rancor.

Ury (1993) and others at the Harvard Negotiation Project have developed methods to support interest-based negotiations. The process described here embeds that wisdom into Adaptive Action and emergent patterns forming in Complex Adaptive Systems.

The most important thing you do in conflict or negotiation situations is to prepare! The first two steps of your Adaptive Action are all about preparation. "If you want a rule of thumb, think about preparing a minute for every minute of interaction with the other side." (Ury, 1993. p16).

"Most negotiations are won or lost even before the talking begins, depending on the quality of the preparation. People who think they can "wing it" without preparing often find themselves sadly mistaken . . . There is no substitute for effective preparation." (Ury, 1993, p. 16).

If you think you're too busy and don't have time to prepare, you are about to make your first and most serious negotiation mistake. Your Adaptive Action cycle to prepare can be done in as little as fifteen minutes. The more complex the issues and negotiation, the longer the preparation should be.

What?

Disruptions in patterns of collaboration and effective shared work can come from a variety of sources.

▶ Conflicting interests
▶ Mismatched levels of power, skill, and information
▶ Incomplete information
▶ Personal histories of hurt or distrust
▶ Different senses of urgency
▶ Resources

As you begin to work on problematic patterns in a collaboration, the first step in your Adaptive Action is to focus on the STAR for the group and to ask **What?**

▶ What are the similarities and differences that can give us strength and coherence together?
▶ What are the differences that could make the whole greater than the sum of the parts?

▶ What are our interactions? How do we talk and listen when we are together?

▶ What is the authentic work we need to do? Is it clear and compelling?

▶ What are the reasons we have for coming together? Do we have a shared understanding of our reasons?

One common barrier to collaboration is the conflict of interests and positions. Your **position** is the **What?** (where you stand, what you identify with, what you say you want). Your **interests** are less tangible; they are the **So What?** (reasons, desires, fears, and aspirations that lead you to take your position). Joint problem-solving revolves around the interests that lie behind each side's positions.

So What?

After you the see the patterns in the current challenge of your collaboration, then it is time to interpret it from multiple perspectives and to explore your options in your **So What?**

So what are possible options? An **option** is a possible agreement or part of an agreement. Devise some options that will satisfy each side's interests. Inventing options for mutual gain is the work of the negotiation. How to do this? Brainstorm multiple options and DO NOT SAY, OR THINK "Well, that won't work." Create several options, invent them first, then evaluate them later.

List all your ideas, then review and evaluate how well they can satisfy your interests and the other side's interests.

So what are our feelings and hopes? It's important to avoid a contest of wills, egos, and power struggles. Nobody wants to feel like they are giving in. One useful approach is to find an independent external standard rather than relying on the will and power of what someone thinks is a useful standard. An independent standard is a benchmark, a measuring stick that is used as a neutral comparison to determine an equitable solution. For example, published market value compared to the argument from one side about financial value in a negotiation. The advantage of independent external standards is that nobody has to feel as if they have to give in to the other.

Think in advance about what might be some independent standards that would appeal to both parties involved in the negotiation. Do your homework, go online and search, be ready. Write a few standards that you think might apply for the main issues.

So what are alternative solutions? If you want to satisfy your interests, it is absolutely critical that you know all the alternatives you have before you begin to negotiate. "The purpose of negotiation is to explore whether you can satisfy your interests better through an agreement than you could by pursuing *Your Best Alternative to a Negotiated Agreement (BATNA)*. Your BATNA is your walk-away alternative. It's the best course of action to satisfying your interests without the other side's agreement in a negotiation. The BATNA defines where you can walk away and be okay. Negotiation is what you do to seek a better solution. Knowing your BATNA is the key to negotiating power. If you have a viable alternative, then you have leverage in the negotiation. The better your BATNA, the more power you have." (Ury, p.22)

Keep your BATNA to yourself and know that if things don't work out you will be okay with it as an acceptable way to meet your interests. Note: Your BATNA should not be hypothetical. It should really exist. It should be as strong as possible, and you must be ready to act on it.

So what do you aspire to? Ask yourself what would be the best outcome for you? For the collaborative work you are doing together? "What would genuinely satisfy your interests and at the same time satisfy enough of the other side's basic concerns that there is at least a chance that they would agree?" (Ury, 1993 p. 25) If you aim too low, you may be dissatisfied. If you aim too high, resolution might be impossible.

These reflections in So What? establish the foundations for the Simple Rules of Now What?

Now What?

No two collaborations are the same, and no two breakdowns are alike, either. You need a path to action that is both reliable and flexible when you are troubleshooting your partnering relationships. On the one hand, you want a reliable process. On the other hand, you want to find a fix that fits the current circumstances. So, what you need are Simple Rules. These are our Simple Rules for negotiation.

▶ Focus on patterns not problems
▶ Stand in inquiry
▶ Set conditions for the future
▶ Appreciate complexity
▶ Iterate and adapt

Focus on Patterns Not Problems

Sometimes this means to step away from the situation so you can see the whole system, as well as your part in it. When the issues are important and the stakes are high, there is often a lot of emotional energy for you and for others. Three common and costly negotiating mistakes made in the heat of the moment are:

▶ Striking back (an eye for an eye, fight fire with fire, give and take, etc.)

▶ Giving in, usually because you're so uncomfortable with what is going on that it's not worth it, and you just want to be done

▶ Breaking off relations with a difficult person or organization (you quit, you walk out, you get a divorce, etc.).

Each of these three reactions results in losing sight of interests. In addition, they give power to the other side and contribute to a harmful action — reaction cycle.

The Adaptive Action/Breakthrough Strategy is to break the cycle, and avoid costly mistakes. Step out of the immediate situation and collect yourself. The metaphor is to imagine that the negotiation is taking place on a stage in a theatre and that you take a time out, leave the stage and go up onto the balcony. You look down upon the stage and now you can see larger patterns that were not visible when you were down on the stage. You calmly re-evaluate the situation as if you were an external observer.

Call "time out" and go to the balcony as often as you need to during negotiation. When you feel the temptation to react, call a timeout. Keep your focus on the shared interests and seek an agreement that is better than your walk-away position (BATNA) and that also meets the other side's interests acceptably.

Stand in Inquiry

Inquiry is as key to *negotiating* as it is to leading and learning. When you work in uncertainty—like every negotiation—your only winning strategy is to ask questions. The other side may display emotions that come out as fear, distrust, and hostility. They may be in a frame of mind such that they refuse to listen to anything you have to say. For them, the world seems "do or die," "eat or be eaten."

Do the opposite of what the other side expects. Resist the temptation to get drawn into their argument. Diffuse their negative energy by taking their side, by listening to them, acknowledging their points and their feelings, agreeing with them and showing them respect.

Sometimes you're dealing with people who seem inflexible and perhaps there is a lot of emotional energy flying about. People are taking sides, feeling distrustful and threatened. At some point we may become convinced that the other side is wrong and that we are right, or vice versa, and stop listening. That is your cue to take a break, go to the balcony and shift away from that constrained and competitive perspective. Now, how can you gain a better perspective and create a favorable climate in which you can both negotiate? That is, find a way to define an open dialogue that continues the play, rather than getting stuck in a dead end, zero-sum relationship, where one or the other of you has to lose. To do this, there needs to be some mutual respect, and respect feeds on inquiry.

When you stand in inquiry, you step to their side. You do three things: listen, acknowledge, agree. Listen to what they have to say. Acknowledge their point, their feelings, and their competence and status. And agree with them wherever you can. ... If you want them to listen to you, begin by listening to them. If you want them to acknowledge your point, acknowledge theirs first. To get them to agree with you, begin by agreeing with them. Try paraphrasing and asking questions. Try to see things from their point of view. Agree whenever you can without conceding. One of my colleagues used to say to the other side, "I agree with you and let me add something..." And then he would go on to rearrange and reframe things. You want to build a working relationship and to avoid taking positions that are adversarial.

Appreciate Complexity

Don't say 'but.' Instead say, "Yes...And" It makes a huge difference, but it is not easy to do; it takes practice. Avoid pointing your finger when you talk and try to use the first-person singular instead of third person singular (I instead of you). "I feel... I get upset when... I'm not comfortable with... The way I see it is." It's much better than, "You never think about anyone else... You broke your word... You're not being clear, etc." (Ury, 1993. pp 52-75).

Complexity offers many different possibilities and reframing is a useful strategy to open up the pattern to help make it more accessible to achieve the goal of joint problem-solving. If the other side takes a polarized position and digs in, you may feel that they are trying to get you to give in, and vice versa. This makes it difficult to get to joint problem-solving. The other side may not know any other way to be. They may view their options as either giving in or defeating you. Accept whatever the other side says for the moment and reframe. For example, "That's interesting, can you tell me more?" "Help me to understand better why that's important for you." In this way, you act on the assumption that your partner is genuinely interested in solving the problem.

Other useful strategies include asking problem-solving questions. For example, "I'm not sure I understand what you're saying. Help me to see why this is important to you," "I think I understand what you're saying, and it would be helpful if you could explain X to me a little bit more." Keep exploring the problem to get to a discussion of their interests instead of their position.

You can also ask, "What if?" questions. You can ask for advice, use open-ended questions. Don't respond when attacked. Rather, reframe the attack to focus the problem and the issues. Easier said than done. The whole idea is to change and reframe the negotiation into a joint problem-solving exercise rather than a back and forth battle of positions and wills. (Ury, 1993. pp 76-104).

Set Conditions for the Future

Think of your negotiation as a dialogue—the purpose of which is to keep the game going. The more you focus on future and future options, the more flexible and grounded you can afford to be. Ury calls this, "Build them a golden bridge." (Ury, 1993. Pp 105) You may have the goal to reach a joint satisfactory solution, however the other side may not be interested in doing this. It may seem as if nothing satisfies them. Perhaps they don't see any benefit for them in finding a joint solution. Maybe they're afraid of losing face, of having to back down or of giving into your ideas.

You support them when you consider the future and build a golden bridge from their position to a mutually satisfactory solution. In a negotiation, there is an identified gap between your interest and theirs. You are working to build a bridge across that gap to achieve a joint solution. The golden bridge helps the other side save face and makes the outcome appear to be a victory for them. When you build a golden bridge, you make it easier for the other side to overcome the obstacles they imagine.

Iterate and Adapt

If the people with whom you are negotiating have a win-lose mentality, then the only thing they will try to do is defeat you, and they will try to use power and deception to do it. They may not be interested in cooperating with you at all.

What if the other side refuses to corporate no matter what you try? They believe they can defeat you in a power game. If you enter this game, it only escalates and often backfires. Instead of using power to escalate, use it to educate. It enhances your negotiating and brings them back to the table because they realize they cannot win by themselves but only together with you. Ask yourself:

▶ What do they know that I need? What do I know that they need?
▶ So what questions can I ask or suggestions can I offer to move the discussion forward?
▶ Now what will I do, and what will I watch for to see if we are moving forward?

Take Adaptive Action to influence outcomes, especially when you cannot predict or control them. Aim for mutual satisfaction instead of victory. The power to iterate and adapt is used to convince the other side that the only way for them to win is for both of you to win together. "Focus their attention on their interests and on avoiding the negative consequences of no agreement... Seek instead to shape their choice so that they make a decision that is in their interest and yours." (Ury, 1993, pp 133)

Of course collaboration is a good thing, and just as certainly, you will run into problems as you build and support collaborative relationships. These Simple Rules for negotiation can help you see, understand, and influence patterns to influence shared understanding and action.

Note—You will work with a group to practice negotiation skills in a case situation. You can choose either *Assessment in a Medical School* or *Quality of Care and Postgraduate Education*. Choose the one that is most useful to you and the work of your team. Follow the instructions in Box 2.3 below

The Triple Bottom Line: Assessment in a Medical School

The Dean (Director) at the medical school at the Superior School of Health Sciences, a well-respected institution, has just returned from the annual deans (directors) meeting where he participated in a workshop on student assessment. He gathers his staff together to share some of what he has learned. He indicates that the medical school needs to reconsider their current student assessment policies and practices. The Dean would like the school to develop and implement an institution-wide assessment program for all courses of study in the medical curriculum so that there is more consistency across all levels of the curriculum and a shared set of underlying assumptions and practices. He also tells them that several other top medical schools are making similar changes and he thinks this new approach to assessment is important for them to sustain their medical school's national reputation and leadership. The Associate Dean for Medical Education is asked to form a representative task force to develop and propose a plan in six months.

A few months later, after many departmental meetings with the Associate Dean and members of the newly formed assessment task force, the chairs (chiefs/heads) of the Departments of Surgery and OB/GYN meet privately with the Dean to object strongly to the time and effort that will be required by their teachers (faculty/staff) to accomplish this proposed work. They feel that it will be too disruptive and take valuable time away from their research and from patient care activities, both of which generate income for the them and the school and sustain the reputation of the institution.

Last week at a meeting of the general curriculum committee, composed of representatives from each department together with the course leaders of the major curriculum blocks and clinical services, there was general support expressed for the new direction of an institution-wide assessment program that would keep educational mission growing and up to date, similar to that of the research and patient care missions of the school.

The Dean has called you in as an outside advisor to help bring these two perspectives closer together and to negotiate an agreement going forward.

The Triple Bottom Line: Quality of Care and Postgraduate Education

A well-known, private Medical School has teaching affiliations at two hospitals in the city. One hospital is public and located in a very poor and violent section of town. Students in the medical school are sent to this hospital to learn clinical skills and see patients as part of their in-hospital and ambulatory clerkship education. The other hospital is private and located in a wealthy part of the city. The medical school sends its postgraduate students (residents) to do their specialty training at this private hospital.

Some parents of the medical students have complained that they don't feel their sons and daughters are safe traveling to and from the public hospital. Furthermore, some students feel that they are being subjected to a poor medical education with poor people. On top of this, some physicians who work in the private hospital don't think it is appropriate for residents who are learning to see their fee-paying patients. Residents have expressed frustration that they are being denied important educational experiences because they are able to see all the patients admitted to the service.

The Dean (Director) and the Chairperson of the Medical School's Education Council call you to help them with these problems

2.3 Practicing Negotiations

Engage with your learning group to respond to the case study.

- ▶ *Decide together, which of the cases you want to focus on.*
- ▶ *Within that case, divide your group in half, one for each of the two sides in the issue. Take time to prepare to negotiate. Each person on a side can take one of the points of view and prepare to represent that point of view in a negotiation session. Review the preparation for negotiation.*
- ▶ *Arrange a day and time for both sides to meet together via telephone or video conference. Plan for a 90-minute conversation.*
- ▶ *Use what you have learned in this Module to explore the issues and come to a mutually agreeable, negotiated solution.*
- ▶ *Share your solution online and compare and contrast your solution to those that other groups found.*
- ▶ *What is similar and different between your group and others?*
- ▶ *What did you learn that you can use in your next negotiation?*

Adaptive Actions

It is great to learn about leadership, but you are taking this course to do more than that. If you want to DO leadership differently, then you have to practice doing leadership differently. That is why each Module of the course includes opportunities for you to practice what you are learning about Adaptive Action, and we will, too.

Our Adaptive Action Assessment and Evaluation

Throughout the course, we are assessing our performance and evaluating the course to be sure we meet your needs. Please help us continually improve this experience by providing feedback on how you are seeing the patterns we wish to create for you and for your learning colleagues. Online you will find a link to an online survey that will invite you to respond to each of these questions and share your insights with us.

Simple Rule	I see this when . . .	I miss this when . . .
Teach and learn in every interaction		
Attend to the whole, the part, and the greater whole		
Give and get value for value		
Search for the true and the useful		
Engage in joyful practice		
Share your leadership story		

Table 6: Our Adaptive Action Module 2: Work Better Together

Your Adaptive Action Experiment

Following the second webinar in the series, you will have two weeks to complete at least one more Adaptive Action Experiment to practice what you have learned and to begin to shift your everyday leadership practice.

For this Module, you will select a Sticky Issue that relates to some kind of collaboration or negotiation that will help people work better together.

Your Adaptive Action Experiment should:

▶ Involve a real-life leadership challenge you face today
▶ Focus on your own Adaptive Action, not on things you wish others would do
▶ Change over time, as you take action to shift it and as you learn more

▶ Stay the same or change during the course
▶ Focus on individual, team, organization, or community patterns

As you focus on this "Sticky Issue," respond to the questions and suggestions in this guide. Capture your reflections in the group discussion, and review and comment on others' Adaptive Action Experiments. The goal of each of your Adaptive Action Experiments is to lead in healthy and sustainable ways to set conditions for others to be successful.

Adaptive Action Experiment 2

Practice what you've learned to build your ability to lead in complex times (Visit the online discussion space to answer any of these questions that are helpful to you. Please keep your response to less than 100 words.)

▶ *What is the pattern you see today?*
Describe your Sticky Issue in three to five sentences. Be as specific and objective as you can be.

▶ *So What does the patterns mean to you and your team? (Here, again, you will use the Pattern Spotters because they help you see what is happening in you Sticky Issue.)*

▷ *So what do you notice in general?*
▷ *So what are exceptions?*
▷ *Are there any contradictions?*
▷ *So what surprises you?*
▷ *So what questions do you have?*

▶ *So What insights can you gain from the models and methods you learned in this Module?*

▶ *Now What will you do to change conditions and shift the pattern?*

Reflecting on Adaptive Action Experiments

Write your reflections, take action, then record your findings. Be prepared to share your experiences verbally, on the online dialogue, or in a written report. Also, review the Adaptive Action Experiments of your group members. Be prepared to give them feedback or ask them questions to help expand or inform their inquiries.

Health and Wellbeing

You cannot set conditions for others to be effective unless you are healthy and strong yourself. One of your most important responsibilities as a leader in a complex system is to take care of yourself, so you have the stamina and energy to serve others.

The models and methods in this Module can help you focus in on your own levels of stress and coping mechanisms. Reflect on the questions below, share your thoughts with your group online, and engage with them in inquiry about how to create patterns of health and wellbeing for yourself and others.

2.4 Your Health and Wellbeing 2

Reflect on these questions and share your thoughts online, if you choose to do so:

:

- ▶ *What patterns emerge from your own, personal complex adaptive system? Emotional? Physical? Social?*
- ▶ *So what patterns from your personal Radical Inquiry support your health and wellbeing?*
- ▶ *So what are your personal Simple Rules and how do they contribute to your health and wellbeing? How do they detract?*
- ▶ *Now what can you do in the next two weeks to become more aware of and shift your patterns of personal health and wellbeing?*
- ▶ *Now what can you do in the next two weeks to influence the health and wellbeing of your team and colleagues?*

Be prepared to share your reflections with your learning group, learning partner, and possibly in the online community.

Summary Work Better Together

Whether you are working with students, other educational colleagues, academic partners, or personal relationships, collaboration sets conditions for new patterns to emerge. In this Module, you explored the potential and challenges of collaborating. You can use Radical Inquiry, Simple Rules, and STAR to set conditions for yourself, your employees, and your students to see, understand, and influence differences to release tension and create new opportunities for effective action. You also practiced using negotiation skills to resolve issues that often make collaboration difficult.

In the next Module, you will encounter a new way to think about "problems" and to measure success for yourself and your community.

Module 3: Find the Fix that Fits

Balancing Freedom and Control

The main challenge of leading in a complex system is that the situation is always changing. That means that you cannot find a single answer or approach that will work all the time. Sometimes, as an effective leader, you have to reach in and take a strong stand. Other times, you should step back and let your team explore and discover their own solutions. To lead in uncertainty, you have to have the capacity to control and to influence conditions, and the wisdom to know when to do which one.

When command and control leadership is called for, it is easy to define and ensure success. In situations of uncertainty, when you can neither command nor control, you have to find new ways to define success and to set conditions for your teams to succeed.

The same challenge affects your role as an educator. Some topics—like basic skills and high-risk procedures—require that you tightly constrain the knowledge and skills of your students. On the other hand, when it comes to questions of judgment, relationship, and complex medical conditions, neither you nor your student can be expected to predict or control outcomes. Still, you are expected to make wise decisions and be accountable for outcomes you cannot control. This Module will help you distinguish between high-control and high-freedom contexts and give you models and methods to help you work effectively in both.

In this Module, we will discuss a way to define and acknowledge success, even when you cannot predict, control, or measure it. This way to think about success gives you freedom, as a leader and trainer, to see patterns more clearly, recognize how they are and are not meeting expectations, and intervene to improve performance—even when no one is keeping score.

That approach is based on finding "fit for function." During this Module, you will:

- ▶ Define success in complex environments
- ▶ Practice Pattern Logic to see, understand, and influence others
- ▶ Use what you have learned in Module 1: Lead in Uncertainty and Module 2: Work Better Together to find what is fit for function
- ▶ Manage paradoxes and dichotomies in your leadership, education, and health care practices
- ▶ Engage in Adaptive Action on your own Sticky Issue

We will review the HSD models and methods you have learned so far, and see what they reveal about adapting your tactics to fit the current environment and the current goals.

Resources for this Module include:

▶ Required readings:
   Review this topic in the Appendices at the back of this book. Use the index in the accompanying book *Adaptive Action: Leveraging Uncertainty in Your Organization* to consider additional perspectives
   ▷ Finite and Infinite Games
   ▷ Pattern Logic
   ▷ Interdependent Pairs
▶ Optional readings:
   ▷ Arrow, H., & Henry, K.B. (2010). Using complexity to promote group learning in healthcare. *J Eval Clin Practice*, 16, 861-866.
   ▷ Cottingham, A.H., Suchman, A. L., Litzelman, D.K., Frankel, R.M., Mossbarger, D.L., Williamson, P.R., . . . Inui, T. S. (2008). Enhancing the informal curriculum of a medical school: a case study in organizational cultural change. *J Gen Intern Med*, 23(6), 715-722.
   ▷ Goldstein, J.A. (1994). The unshackled organization: facing the challenge of unpredictability through spontaneous reorganization. Portland: Productivity Press.
   ▷ Guastello, S.J. (2010). Self-organization and leadership emergence in emergency response teams. *Nonlinear Dynamics, Psychology, and Life Sciences Psychology, and Life Sciences*, 14(2), 179-204.
▶ Other resources:
   ▷ Live Virtual Workshop on Interdependent Pairs, HSD Institute

This Module includes the following sections:

▶ Success Is . . .
▶ Excellent Enough
▶ Pattern Logic
▶ Patterns of Constraint
▶ Finding the Fit for Function

> The definition of success in medical education has changed over the years. For students, the concept of success has evolved from being able to replicate memorized facts and being an independent solo practitioner to being adept at sensing context in making meaning of incomplete information and being versatile in teams and collaboration. In addition, there is now much more emphasis on ethics, professionalism, and communication with patients and colleagues than there was fifty years ago.

Success Is . . .

Sometimes it is useful to think about success in terms of winning and losing a game. In a Complex Adaptive System (CAS) there are two kinds of games and two very different ways to win.

A CAS can give you a Finite Game, like soccer or basketball. It has:

▶ Clear boundaries
▶ Explicit beginning and ending
▶ Rules and scorekeeping
▶ Team and opponents

The purpose of the Finite Game is to win.

Some of the work you do as a leader and a teacher are Finite Games. Acute care, multiple-choice examinations, budgets, best practices, and most management/union negotiations are all examples of human Complex Adaptive Systems. They are clear, and success is easy to see and measure. You can define the task, prepare, recognize and measure performance, do everything well, and win the game. It is straightforward to play Finite Games and to teach others how to play them.

You have had lots of practice playing Finite Games, and you have also succeeded in teaching others how to play them. When you are engaged in a Finite Game, you:

▶ Set clear goals
▶ Monitor performance
▶ Provide incentives
▶ Define regulations and best practices
▶ Build protocols and checklists
▶ Expect reliability and accountability

The problem in an uncertain environment is that these tactics may not help at all. Sometimes, the complex system has another game in mind. It is an Infinite Game. Most of your Sticky Issues arise from Infinite Games. Chronic illness, end of life care, raising children, and marriage are good examples of Infinite Games. (For more information refer to Appendix 3). They have:

▶ Ambiguous and/or flexible boundaries
▶ No clear starting point and no clear end
▶ The rules keep changing
▶ There are many ways to keep score
▶ Allies become opponents (or opponents become allies) unexpectedly

The purpose of the Infinite Game is to keep the game going, to keep playing. When you play an Infinite Game well, you will:

▶ Stand in inquiry
▶ Look for patterns
▶ Use Adaptive Action to experiment until you find what works

Every day, you are invited to play innumerable games. Some of them are Finite Games, some are Infinite Games, and still others can be played as one or the other—you choose. Some of the work you do can only be played as an Infinite Game. One of your roles as leader is to define which kind of game you and your team are playing. Only then can you determine what success looks like, how to get it, and what is a reasonable investment.

3.1 Your Finite and Infinite Games

Reflect on these questions and share your thoughts online (less than 25 words):

> ▶ *What Infinite Games influence your Sticky Issue? What Finite ones?*
> ▶ *So what does success look like, if you think of the Finite Game? The Infinite?*
> ▶ *Now what can you do to set conditions to help your team be successful in every game they play?*

Excellent Enough

If you are playing a Finite Game you can be certain about what is supposed to happen. Often you have seen the problem before and know what to expect. If so, then success is easy to define and measure. In this course, we look at the challenges that are much more complex, uncertain, and unpredictable. Examples include building clinical relationships; working with chronic illness or difficult staff members; engaging with community; finding an instructional approach that will work for everyone, all the time; and planning for one hundred years into the future.

As a leader and an educator, you are responsible for these and for many other situations where simple goals and measures are not meaningful. More than that, inappropriate measures can do harm, if they are applied carelessly when they are not "fit for function."

We use the term "fit for function" to describe success in situations that are Infinite Games: Open, difficult to describe, and massively entangled with other complex situations and processes. It means that an action or decision:

▶ Reflects what is currently known about the situation
▶ Works across scales—individuals, teams, organization, community
▶ Moves the system toward its ultimate goal
▶ Empowers those who and should act to shift the pattern

You cannot know ahead of time if the action is the best of all possible choices. A choice that is fit for function may or may not be perfect. You may find information in the future that would have led to a different conclusion. It may not match your expectations or the expectation of others, but it is excellent enough to move you and your system forward in the direction of your goals. If you are accustomed to being in charge, if you expect yourself always to pick the right answer, if you think you can and should always know what is best, then you will not be satisfied with this measure of success. We have lots of empathy for you, but we can assure you: in complex and uncertain situations, fit for function is the only reasonable measure of success.

When answers can be known, when success can be measured, then know it and measure it. But, when you are working in emergent authentic situations, where uncertainty is the only certainty, then turn your eyes to a different standard, and find what is fit for function. Find what is excellent enough to move you, your team, and your patients forward.

Pattern Logic

Because of the complexity of Infinite Games and Sticky Issues, it is impossible to have a total understanding of a situation. There is no way to find a "root cause." There are many causes that are at work at the same time, and some of them are quite confusing because they are both causes and effects. For example, high levels of MRSA infection are a result of many different things, and as the number of infections increases, the risks of infection increase as well. The spread becomes exponential because it is driven by a nonlinear feedback loop. This complex causality is common in Infinite Games, so traditional analytical processes are often not successful. (For more information, refer to Appendix 3.)

When causality is unknowable, your traditional problem-solving methods do not work. You cannot divide the problem up into parts. You cannot predict the future or control what will happen. You cannot define best practices or replicate solutions in diverse environments. The best you can do is to use Adaptive Action to explore and create opportunities for action. HSD offers another tool to help you work in such unpredictable and chaotic environments. It will help you 1) Name dominant patterns in your system; 2) Identify a set of conditions that seem to have influenced those patterns; 3) Take informed action as you look for ways to change the conditions and shift the patterns; then 4) Watch to see if the patterns have shifted, learn what you can, and begin your next Adaptive Action cycle.

HSD has defined this ability to see, understand, and influence patterns that emerge in Complex Adaptive Systems and Infinite Games as Pattern Logic.

Figure 9: Pattern Logic

Pattern Logic: *Seeing, understanding, and influencing similarities, differences, and connections that affect change in the part, whole, and greater whole of a complex system.*

Patterns are similarities, differences, and connections that have meaning across space and time. Pattern Logic is seeing patterns that emerge in a changing context and making logical decisions based on the dynamics of that perceived pattern.

Pattern Logic helps you make sense of your world and helps you make excellent enough leadership choices. If you are playing a Finite Game, where you can be in control and predict the future, you will find lots of similarities, few differences, and tight connections. For example, in acute care situations, patterns are clear and behaviors are constrained. Patients are sorted by ailment, job descriptions are clear and constraining, protocols are defined, and quality can be easily measured. When this is the case you can:

► Know what is the right thing to do
► Use best practices
► Hold people absolutely accountable for outcomes
► Expect quick and accurate responses to requests
► Be in control
► Avoid surprises

Sometimes the patterns in the Complex Adaptive System are not so clear. Then you play the Infinite Game. Weak boundaries, few similarities, many differences, and weak connections mean that you have little if any control over what happens. The system is unconstrained, and anything can happen. Delivering care, teaching, and/or leading in primary care situations are all examples of Infinite Games, with loosely coupled connections. Patterns are unclear, changing all the time, and dependent on factors you cannot know or control. When you are in these situations, where traditional management techniques do not work, you can use Adaptive Action and Pattern Logic together to help you find an excellent enough path of action.

▶ **What?** See current patterns clearly by asking:
  ▷ What is the same?
  ▷ What is different?
  ▷ What is connected and how?

▶ **So what?** Understand the significance of the pattern and whether or not it is fit for function by asking:
  ▷ So what are the tensions held in differences in the system?
  ▷ So what are the constraints?
  ▷ So what is possible?
  ▷ So what is my ability to predict and control?
  ▷ So what are multiple perspectives about what is same, different, or connected?

▶ **Now what?** Take action, in the moment, to shift the conditions and influence the pattern by:
  ▷ Now what will change the similarities to increase or decrease constraint to be more fit for function?
  ▷ Now what will shift the differences to change the constraint to be more fit for function?
  ▷ Now what connections will influence the amount of constraint or freedom in the system?

In general, Pattern Logic can give you hints about what to do to improve fit for function, whether you are leading, teaching, or healing.

▶ When things are the same, they tend to stick together and to be stable, but too much similarity drives the energy out of the system. If you want to increase control, focus on the ways that things are the same.

▶ When things are different, they hold tension and potential for change. Too much difference means that patterns cannot form or be sustained, but too little difference locks the system in place. If you want to increase control, focus in on just a few differences. If you want to increase freedom, expand the list of differences that make a difference.

▶ When things are connected, change can move from one part of the system to another. Very tight connections mean more predictability and control. Weaker connections mean more freedom and creativity. Increase the number or strength of connections to gain control, and reduce them to reduce constraint and increase freedom.

The models, methods, and practices you learn in this course will help you use Pattern Logic to see what is happening more clearly, to understand your options, to choose a "next wise action," to watch how the patterns shift in response, and to being the next cycle of observation and action.

This brief case study will demonstrate how Adaptive Action and Pattern Logic work together to help you work with Infinite Games.

Jack's Dead and the boys have gone (from Sweeny, 2006. Complexity in Primary Care. Radcliff;Oxford. Pp.3-4)

Some years ago our practice nurse asked me to see Mrs. B, 85-year-old widow who as I recall, at the time of consultation, had been registered as a patient with me for about 15 years. I knew her well. Her husband, a pleasant chap who had been a builder, had died five years previously. Mrs. B was pretty much estranged from her two grown sons, who were recurrent petty criminals, both serving prison sentences at the time of the consultation. Box 1.1 shows the conditions from which Mrs. be suffered and Box 1.2 shows her test results, which the nurse wanted me to review with her.

Mrs. B's comorbidity	When we met, at the practice nurse's request, I rehearsed the abundant evidence supporting interventions to lower blood pressure, to improve the control of her diabetes and reduce her lipid levels. I remember even thinking where the references for this all lay (with a résumé in Clinical Evidence).
Diabetes	
Hypertension	
Osteoarthritis	
Macular degeneration	
Hallus valgus	

I confess to feeling just a shade confident as I explained the abnormalities and how we could 'help' to reduce her risk. After a few moments I stopped - resting my case, as a barrister might say. Mrs. B remained silent for a moment or two. Then she said, "Well, Jack's dead and the boys have gone. ... At the simplest level, one can say that the consultation, at the point when Mrs. B made this contribution, moved from being doctor-centered to patient-centered. It moved, one could say, from the biomedical domain to the biographical domain, or from clinical, evidence-based medicine to a consultation predicated on narrative-based evidence

---

But the shift was profound. When the consultation moved from its biomedical phase, it shed its parameters of P-values, absolute risk and numbers needed to treat. These were replaced by the parameters of the biographical

Mrs. B's test results	
Glycosylated hemoglobin	9.7%
Blood pressure mmHg	180/96
Total cholesterol	8.8 mmol/l
Body mass index	29 kg/m2

phase of the consultation led by Mrs. B. Here despair, hopelessness, regret, guilt perhaps, and defeat were the parameters. Physical parameters had been replaced by metaphysical ones-two intellectual worlds seem to have collided. ...It is clear that, when Mrs. B offered her contribution, the consultation took off in another direction. Up until that point, a fairly straightforward consultation was proceeding, drawing on scientific evidence gleaned from good clinical trials, many of them randomized and controlled, in the great tradition of scientific medicine.

The remainder of the consultation, led by Mrs. B, had nothing to do with that way of thinking and arose from her lived experience. Yet in that context Mrs. B's narrative evidence had more impact on the outcome of the interaction between Mrs. B and myself than the clinical evidence-based observations with which I led the consultation. There were, one could argue, two ways of explaining things which were competing for influence-two explanatory models which at first sight did not seem to overlap much. At a deeper level, there were two types of knowledge jostling to influence. Two different types of viewing and making sense of the world were at stake."

3.2 Patterns of Your Team

Reflect on these questions and share your thoughts online (less than 25 words):

▶ **What similarities hold your team together?**
▶ **What differences inspire their innovation and/or conflict?**
▶ **What connections do they form inside and outside of work, and how do those connections influence performance?**

Patterns of Constraint

All of the models and methods you have learned in this course can help you find solutions that are fit for function and to help you help others do the same thing. The following table outlines the models and gives examples of what would and would not be fit for function as you look through each lens.

Model & Method	High Constraint High Certainty Control	Low Constraint Little Certainty Influence	Useful When
CAS (Complex Adaptive Systems)	Few agents Very homogeneous Tight connections Sharp patterns Lots of agreement	Many agents High diversity Loose connections Fuzzy patterns No agreement	Teams Communities Silo-busting Quality control Stakeholder groups
Adaptive Action	Fast cycles High agreement Precise data Clear questions Predictable results	Slow cycles Many perspectives Missing data Exploration Unknowable results	Feeling stuck Individual choices Collaborative acts Uncertainty Learning
Pattern Logic	Strong identity Clear boundaries Few differences Tight exchanges	Ambiguous roles Interdependencies Many differences Loose connections	Inter-professional Negotiations Co-creation New processes
Simple Rules	Few and meaningful Shape patterns Easy to remember Create positive future	Many Not agreed Different expectations Divided action	New teams Collaborations Culture change Onboarding staff
Radical Inquiry	Clear identity Shared values Good communication	Personal stories Autonomy Freedom Creativity	Building a team Creating a culture Clarifying roles Setting expectations
STAR	More same than different Power relationships Clear work Shared reason	More different than same Weak relationships Big or fuzzy work Different agendas	Co-creation Effective work team Resolving conflicts Begin collaboration

Table 7: Fit or Not Fit for Function

You can use this table to assess performance and success as fit for function whenever you are in a situation where measures are either impossible or unrealistic. If you find that the current situation is not fit for function, then you can use the same models and methods to help nudge the system toward greater fit.

The work of Holly Arrow and Kelly Henry (2010) (see the references in this Module) shows an innovative approach to measuring success among different operating room teams learning minimally invasive cardiac surgery. "All teams in the study completed the same three-day training programme, and all found learning the process challenging, as the technique requires high levels of both vigilance and flexibility. Some teams learned effectively. Others failed to improve with experience. One surgeon reported that 'after fifty cases…I'm not getting that much better.' Among more successful teams, one in particular both mastered the technique and also continued learning from visitors who came through the hospital. 'It's amazing what you can learn from them if you listen. Even people who've done a few cases have ideas'." Three factors predicted success: "… the ease with which team members spoke up during operations, the amount of boundary spanning communication with other hospital groups, and the extent to which the surgeons acted as coaches for their teams. All three factors boosted the flow of energy and information within the group, moving it into a more productive dynamic state." (p.861).

You have some key questions that will lead to success. They are very simple, though not easy: Is this solution fit for function? Is this solution excellent enough to lead us into our next Adaptive Action cycle?

Many leadership programs, pedagogies, and change methodologies focus on common interests and shared goals, but they are not always possible in complex environments. If you wait for a collaborative relationship to define a shared vision, you may never get shared work off the ground. So, in HSD, we find it helpful to focus on differences. In a CAS, differences hold the tension in the system. They are the potential energy to move the pattern to be more fit for function. We use Interdependent Pairs to see and talk about differences that make a difference.

Tension in the Extremes

Interdependent Pairs is a model and method that allows individuals and groups to explore the paradoxes that emerge from the complexity in their systems. In a complex system, there is very little that is all or nothing. The challenges that have you stuck are the ones where there is no clear one-way consideration. The stickiness of your issues comes because you move on shifting landscapes between the extreme positions on the questions you face. (For more information refer to Appendix 3.)

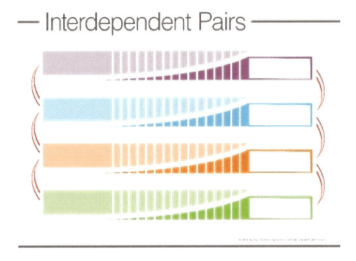

Figure 10: Interdependent Pairs

Interdependent Pairs: Dichotomies that capture the underlying tensions in any system. They are paradoxes that can either build energy or stop forward progress.

Finding the Fit

Interdependent Pairs help you see and respond to find the fit as you engage with students, patients, collaborations, teams, and programs. They inform your Adaptive Action.

What? In our experience, unstable or unpredictable situations emerge from a framework of Interdependent Pairs. Barry Johnson (1992), in his *Handbook of Polarity Management: Identifying and Managing Unsolvable Problems*, describes these pairs as polarities. In medical education and in leadership, some key Interdependent Pairs are:

▶ Individual contribution and group performance
▶ Best practices and local adaptation
▶ Acute care and chronic care
▶ Safety and freedom of choice
▶ Cost, quality outcomes, and patient experience

In a complex system, multiple polarities are at play at the same time, and they interact to make things even more complicated. Rarely do you operate at either extreme end of any pair.

In less complex times, you could use phrases like "either/or" to describe a challenge or a decision. Then there was recognition of the interdependent nature of some of these extremes in these polarities, and the movement was toward using "both/and" language. In highly complex systems, however, the more realistic picture is that the final critical factor actually moves along a continuum between the two extremes. The next wise action for anyone is dependent upon the unique factors present in a given situation. Additionally, in complex systems, another source of uncertainty lies in the fact that multiple polarities exist and are interdependent with each other. A movement along one pair to resolve one challenge can lead to radical transformation along another pair and create new, unintended challenges.

An example will illustrate how Interdependent Pairs can find simple patterns in complex situations. Many issues can influence a labor/management negotiation. Pay, safety, benefits, working conditions, seniority, and historical relationships are all factors that play a part in setting and resolving interests and positions. When these differences are all mixed up, the conversation jumps from one place to another and, generally, stays stuck. On the other hand, if each of the Interdependent Pairs can be defined, then the pattern of dialogue can be clarified and simplified.

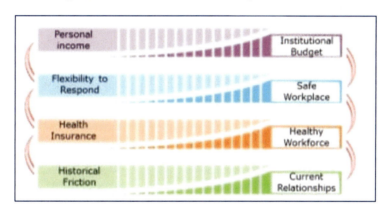

Figure 11: Tensions in Negotiations

When the negotiation is framed in this way it is easier for both sides to see what they are asking for and offering in return.

So What? You can use this model and method to explore the Interdependent Pairs that contribute to the Sticky Issues of your leadership and teaching. By looking at the dynamics of the patterns that shape your greatest challenges, you can identify the factors that are at play and the degree to which they influence each other.

Now What? So when you feel stuck in your next challenge—and you cannot see your next step, use Interdependent Pairs as a model to help you see where you are stuck and as a method to help you identify your next step.

What are the sticking points that seem intractable? Where is the tension in the system preventing movement? Which of those points seem to be in direct competition or contradiction to each other? Where and how are those points interdependent with each other and with other points of tension you see?

▶ So what can you do to find the balance between the Interdependent Pairs you see? What wise action will leverage the points to your greatest advantage?

▶ Now what action can you take to resolve the tension and move forward?

For decades, the tension has been growing between medical teachers who believed that theory or practice should come first. Some believe that students had to first learn the basics, the core vocabulary of the sciences such as anatomy, physiology, biochemistry, pathology, microbiology, and pharmacology. Then they could work and learn meaningfully in clinical settings and with clinical cases. Years of study support the opposite view. Comparisons with student learning of both the clinical and basic sciences in small-groups (e.g., team-based learning and problem-based learning) have demonstrated that students can learn the sciences basic to medicine in the context of well-defined clinical problems.

There remain tensions about how much practical experience and when it should happen in the whole scheme of medical education. What are optimal settings for authentic clinical learning? There is no fixed solution, and every medical school does it differently. In general, there is a global movement toward increasing students' engagement in small-group learning with clinical contexts. There is still a long way to go and many traditional teachers remain skeptical, especially in cultures and places where there is a strong belief in tradition and hierarchy in health care and health professional education.

Adaptive Actions

Our Adaptive Action

Throughout the course, we are assessing our performance and evaluating the course to be sure we meet your needs. Please help us continually improve this experience by providing feedback on how you are seeing the patterns we wish to create for you and your learning colleagues.

We use the HSD Simple Rules (in column one below) to guide our work in human systems dynamics and in the development, implementation, and evaluation of this course. After each Module, you will visit an online survey to capture your evaluation of your performance and of the course as you respond to these questions.

Simple Rule	I see this when . . .	I miss this when . . .
Teach and learn in every interaction		
Attend to the whole, the part, and the greater whole		
Give and get value for value		
Search for the true and the useful		
Engage in joyful practice		
Share your leadership story		

Table 8: Our Adaptive Action Module 3: Find the Fix that Fits

Your Adaptive Action Experiment

Following the third webinar in the series, you will have two weeks to complete at least one Adaptive Action Experiment to practice what you have learned and to begin to shift your everyday leadership practice.

For this Module, you will select a Sticky Issue that relates to finding a fix that fits your particular situation.

Your Adaptive Action Experiment should:

▶ Involve a real-life leadership challenge you face today
▶ Focus on your own Adaptive Action, not on things you wish others would do
▶ Change over time, as you take action to shift it and as you learn more
▶ Stay the same or change during the course
▶ Focus on individual, team, organization, or community patterns

As you focus on this "Sticky Issue," respond to the questions and suggestions in this guide. Capture your reflections in the group discussion and review and comment on others' Adaptive Action Experiments. The goal of each of your Adaptive Action Experiments is to lead in healthy and sustainable ways to set conditions for others to be successful.

Adaptive Action Experiment 3

Practice what you've learned to build your ability to lead in complex times (Visit the online discussion space to answer any of these questions that are helpful to you. Please keep your response to less than 100 words.)
▶ *What is the pattern you see today?*
  Describe your Sticky Issue in three to five sentences. Be as specific and objective as you can be.
▶ *So What does the patterns mean to you and your team? (By now you should be familiar with the Pattern Spotters. How have you found them useful in other applications?)*
  ▷ *So what do you notice in general?*
  ▷ *So what are exceptions?*
  ▷ *Are there any contradictions?*
  ▷ *So what surprises you?*
  ▷ *So what questions do you have?*
▶ *So What insights can you gain from the models and methods you learned in this Module?*
▶ *Now What will you do to change conditions and shift the pattern?*

Reflecting on Adaptive Action Experiments

Write your reflections, take action, then record your findings. Be prepared to share your experiences verbally, on the online dialogue, or in a written report to submit to the faculty for review. Also, review the Adaptive Action Experiments of your group members. Be prepared to give them feedback or ask them questions to help expand or inform their inquiries.

Health and Wellbeing

You cannot set conditions for others to be effective unless you are healthy and strong yourself. One of your most important responsibilities as a leader in a complex system is to take care of yourself, so you have the stamina and energy to serve others.

The models and methods in this Module can help you focus in on your own levels of stress and coping mechanisms. Reflect on the questions below, share your thoughts with your group online, and engage with them in inquiry about how to create patterns of health and wellbeing for yourself and others.

3.3 Your Health and Wellness 3

Reflect on these questions and share your thoughts online, if you choose to do so:

▶ *What patterns emerge from your own, personal Complex Adaptive System? Emotional? Physical? Social?*

▶ *So what are your personal emotional and physical responses to each zone on the Landscape?*

▶ *So where are you now? How can you move to a zone that is more healthful for you?*

▶ *Now what can you do in the next two weeks to become more aware of and shift your patterns of personal health and wellbeing?*

▶ *Now what can you do in the next two weeks to influence the health and wellbeing of your team and colleagues?*

▶ *Now what will you do to continue these practices to support yourself after the course is complete?*

Summary Find the Fix that Fits

In this Module you redefined success in a complex system. While you can still play the Finite Game to win, you can also engage with Infinite Games to improve performance and outcomes when you cannot predict what will happen or control the environment. By using Interdependent Pairs, you can see the current situation clearly, you can understand the benefits and challenges of the current state, and you can take immediate and intentional action to make a difference today and for the future.

Module 4: Make the Good Better

Assessing Performance and Evaluating Programs

In your leadership role, you plan for, design, develop, support, implement, and/or monitor programs for student assessment and program evaluation. In many ways, you are engaged in both assessment (judging the performance of individual students) and evaluation (judging the effectiveness and efficiency of programs).

Many people think of traditional assessment and evaluation activities as summative—they happen at the end of a process, and the goal is to judge whether the performance or outcomes were good enough. While that may be useful, we do not believe it is the primary purpose for collecting and analyzing data and providing results. We believe that both leadership and learning require a different kind of engagement. We think that both should be formative. They should be designed to improve performance and to make the good better.

Others focus on quantitative indicators and measures to determine success. While we believe those are important, we also find them insufficient to capture the complex emerging learning of individuals and the emerging patterns of programs. We will share with you here some methods you can use to see, understand, and influence patterns of student and program performance that reach beyond the limits of standardized testing and quantitative analysis.

In this Module, you will explore this vision of formative assessment, evaluation, and practice, and you will apply this view to your leadership issues with evaluation and assessment. You will:

▶ Explore multiple approaches to leading assessment and evaluation activities

▶ Explore how evaluation approaches can inform how you lead learning and quality improvement

▶ Base your use of assessment processes on principles of practice to integrate learning and performance

▶ Lead systems of evaluation (Adaptive Action) to sustain patterns of successful performance

▶ Help your students, and those you lead, create and maintain systems to assess and improve their own performance

Resources for this Module include:

▶ Required readings:
Review this topic in the Appendices at the back of this book. Use the index in the accompanying book *Adaptive Action: Leveraging Uncertainty in Your Organization* to consider additional perspectives.
  ▷ Landscape Diagram

▶ Optional readings:
  ▷ Epstein, R. M., Dannefer, E.F., Jospe, N., Nofziger, A.C., Connard, L. W., Hansen, J.T., . . . Henson, L. C. (2004). Comprehensive assessment of professional competence: The Rochester experiment. *Teaching and Learning in Medicine*, 16(1), 186-196.
  ▷ Frank, J.R., Snell, L., Sherbino, J. (eds.). (2015) CanMEDS 2015 Physician Competency Framework. Ottawa:Royal College of Physicians and Surgeons of Canada. Retrieved September 7, 2016, from http://www.royalcollege.ca/rcsite/canmeds/canmeds-framework-e
  ▷ Johnson, B. (1992). Polarity management: identifying and managing unsolvable problems. Amherst, MA: HRD Press.
  ▷ Patton, MQ. (1997). *Utilization-focused evaluation* (3rd ed.). Thousand oaks: Sage.
  ▷ Schuwirth, L.W.T., & van der Vleuten, C.P.M. (2004). Changing education, changing assessment, changing research? *Medical Education*, 38, 805-812.
  ▷ Patton, M.Q. (2011). Developmental Evaluation: Applying complexity concepts to enhance innovation and use. New York: The Guilford Press.
  ▷ Schuwirth, L., & Ash, J. (2013). Assessing tomorrow's learners: incompetency-based education only a radically different holistic method of assessment will work. Six things we could forget. *Medical Teacher*, 35, 555-559.
  ▷ Schuwirth, L.W.T., & van der Vleuten, C.P.M. (2004). Changing education, changing assessment, changing research? *Medical Education, 38*, 805-812.
  ▷ Schuwirth, L., & van der Vleuten, C.P.M. (2011). Programmatic assessment: From assessment of learning to assessment for learning. *Medical Teacher*, 33, 478-485
  ▷ Van Der Vleuten, Cees P. M., & Dannefer, E.F. (2012). Towards a systems approach to assessment. *Medical Teacher*, 34, 185-186.

▶ Other resources:
  ▷ Evaluative Inquiry for Complex Times, Beverly Parsons
  ▷ Designing Initiative Evaluation, The Kellogg Foundation
  ▷ Leadership as Fit Assessment, HSD Institute
  ▷ Seven Zones of Leadership, Robert Terry

> **4.1 Your Assessment and Evaluation Experience**
>
> **Reflect on these questions and share your thoughts online (fewer than 25 words):**
> - ► **What challenges do you currently face as you lead systems that are involved with student assessment and/or program evaluation?**
> - ► **So what is working and what might be more effective?**
> - ► **Now what questions do you have about this process that might improve your performance and the performance of your students and staff?**

In this Module, you will explore:

- ► Judging the Better and the Worse
- ► Evaluating in Uncertainty
- ► Good, Better, Best

Judging the Better and the Worse

In leadership, as in medicine and teaching, you manage systems that help you and others have the ability to tell the better from the worse. Even if there isn't a perfect single correct answer, you have to provide support for people to give their best. For example, when you have been working with a resident/house officer, and he or she is prepared to assume selected responsibilities for patient care and/or ready to complete advanced studies, it is your responsibility to determine readiness or your responsibility to support others who will make that recommendation. That moment should be just the same as every moment of previous engagement with the student. Processes and practices throughout your programs should reinforce the importance of evaluative, systemic thinking. At every point, your programs should be asking whether the student is ready for the next challenge. And, if not, what you and they can do to get ready.

There was a student in a small problem-based learning group who consistently assessed herself as more prepared and more capable than I thought she was. The group had agreed upon criteria for success when we began working together. At every group session we did self, peer, and facilitator/preceptor feedback and assessment. She consistently fell short of expectations, but there was always some real-life reason for her incomplete or not quite acceptable performance. The other members of the group wanted to support her as they felt she was trying very hard with significant challenges at home. The group wanted to ignore the issues of not being prepared so they could support their friend and colleague. While she and they continued to promise that her performance would improve, she continued to miss deadlines and submit sub-standard work.

When we discussed this at the halfway point, she promised to improve. By the end of the unit, she still had not performed according to criteria. Throughout the course, I had kept notes and feedback to support my assessment. She knew about my assessment, but she disagreed. In a tense exchange she said, "Well, that's your opinion." I said, "Yes, that is correct. There is evidence to support my opinion, and I am recommending what would be most helpful for you at this time."

She had received feedback about her performance all along the way and kept making excuses. The students in the group felt sorry for her. I had the responsibility to tell her that her work needed to be better to pass the unit. She disagreed and felt that I was discriminating against her. We sought mediation with the result that she had to take time out from school and then return at a time when she could devote more attention to her studies.

That is what it means to participate in continuous processes of collecting information, judging performance, and taking action to reinforce and to correct. Sometimes it is more difficult than you expect. Adaptive Action is the most effective way we have found to implement this process of being a critical and inquisitive friend everywhere and all the time.

When it comes to program/curriculum evaluation, you want to be sure that the program meets the needs and works within the constraints of the situation. Effective evaluation:

- ▶ E-value-ates, as you test to see if the programs reflect your values
- ▶ Improves design and implementation of learning and programs
- ▶ Ensures that programs meet needs and objectives
- ▶ Generates and uses evidence-based practice when appropriate
- ▶ Learns from the past to inform the future
- ▶ Demonstrates return on investment to increase resources

When these questions become the *What* and the *So What* of your Adaptive Action, then you will be seeing what you need to see and making the changes you need to make.

Student assessment processes follow the same design as any other Adaptive Action. The student's readiness and performance are assessed against agreed upon and known criteria and models. Options are identified about ways to help the student improve. Finally, feedback is provided to move them along toward better performance. Successful assessment processes:

► Provide feedback to help them see the areas in need of improvement and agree upon actions to help them get better
► Inform individual inquiry and self-reflection for their learning
► Approve and certify completion of goals and objectives
► Learn how to make the conditions for performance better

Evaluating in Uncertainty

All of the models and methods you have learned so far in this course can help you see, understand, and influence performance for both programs and students. Use this section of the guide to reflect on how you might integrate each of them into your own assessment and evaluation programs. We will explore each of these models separately and how you might incorporate them into effective student assessment and program evaluation systems for your institution.

Complex Adaptive Systems (CAS)

The primary role of a leader is to set conditions for others to create patterns of successful performance. In complex systems, you can expect that diverse factors and agents interact as patterns of performance arise. You can use the process of Complex Adaptive Systems to assess or evaluate unpredictable, patterned behavior. Systems that support student assessment using CAS, might focus on the following Adaptive Action questions:

► What changes do I observe in knowledge? In skills? In attitudes?
► So what patterns are emerging for this student over time?
► Now what conditions are barriers and/or bridges to patterns of improved performance?

In the context of program evaluation, the CAS model can also be quite informative. In this Adaptive Action, a program might ask:

► What are the agents, interactions, and emerging patterns within and beyond this program?
► So what is working well? What is not? Where are there tensions, and to what extent are the tensions constructive or destructive?
► Now what changes in agents and interactions will create a different, and more productive, pattern?

When you conceive of performance as a pattern that emerges from complex interactions, then you begin to re-think what it means to teach, to lead, and to practice medicine. You suddenly have many options for action where you previously saw few or none.

Adaptive Action

You can think of any evaluative process as an engagement of Adaptive Action. The purpose, after all, is to collect data (What?), consider its value and worth (So What?), and inform future action (Now What?).

Consider the Adaptive Actions cycles in every evaluative or assessment system you design or support, every leadership conversation you engage in, and every opportunity you have to improve your own skills.

When you use Adaptive Action for assessing student performance, progress, or readiness to step into the next level of action. You might ask some of the following questions:

▶ What are the places where the student gets stuck in his or her own Adaptive Action cycles with individual or team work? Clinical or administrative? Theoretical or practical?
▶ So what opportunities exist for changing conditions and improving performance?
▶ Now what are expectations for the next cycle of Adaptive Action?

In program evaluation, you and your teams will also find Adaptive Action an efficient and effective way to approach decision making and action taking. You can ask:

▶ Where are individuals and groups using Adaptive Action?
▶ So what gets the program stuck?
▶ Now what can be done to move it forward?

Continuous cycles of Adaptive Action for individuals, teams, programs, and institutions will continuously "make the good better."

Pattern Logic (CDE Model)

Pattern Logic focuses on how things are the same, different, or connected, so it can be a powerful model for considering and improving performance for individuals, programs, or processes. If you consider performance to be a pattern, then questions about pattern coherence and pattern tensions become natural and very, very productive.

CDE Model refers to the conditions that influence the behavior of self-organizing systems. Patterns in complexity are captured as conditions that show the pattern and also determine how it emerges over time. In the CDE, C stands for container, or the aspects of the system that hold it together. D stands for the differences that influence the pattern now and set conditions for the pattern to change in future. E stands for exchange that connect parts of the system together and let them influence each other.

When your relationships or processes engage in student assessment, ask:

▶ What are current patterns of performance?

▶ How are the current patterns of performance similar to, different from, and connected to the patterns of excellence we aspire to?

▶ Now what can be done to shift the pattern to be more fit for function?

Patterns can also be quite useful in judging the value and worth of programs in evaluation programs as well. You might ask:

▶ How is this program similar to our expectations? Different? Connected?

▶ So what tensions currently exist?

▶ Now what will change the conditions to influence the constraints and shift the pattern to reach the objectives of the program?

Pattern Logic opens a non-judgmental, flexible, complex assessment, and evaluation approach that meets the requirements of flexible and complex environments and requirements. You can use it either in formal design of assessment or evaluation or informally as you pursue your other leadership challenges.

Simple Rules

Simple Rules are powerful foundations for assessment and for evaluation. Because they influence the behavior that creates patterns of desired performance, you can use them as an entire evaluative framework. You can establish a rubric—table of levels of performance—to organize data, analyze findings, and promote corrective action.

When you use Simple Rules for student assessment, you can ask:

▶ What evidence of the Simple Rules do you see in the student's behavior?

▶ So what are the consequences of fidelity or mismatch between the rules and current behavior?

▶ Now what rules, behaviors, patterns can be shifted to improve performance?

Simple Rules are powerful ways to evaluate program performance, as well. You can ask:

▶ What are the current Simple Rules of the group?

▶ So what does high, medium, low performance look like on each rule?

▶ Now what will move the pattern of performance up?

Simple Rules are an efficient and effective way to identify expectations and to communicate them in a way that is clear and actionable.

Radical Inquiry

Usually we use Radical Inquiry to begin the process of design or implementation of an assessment or evaluation process. The questions involved in Radical Inquiry help individuals and groups engage in an active way with what they want to achieve and what they collectively see as their assets and areas in need of improvement.

In the context of individual or team assessment, you can ask:

▶ What pattern is ideal? What pattern do you want to create?

▶ So what identity, measures of difference, and modes of connection will contribute to that ideal pattern?

▶ Now what supports will be required to set conditions for the ideal pattern to emerge?

Program evaluation is a particularly powerful place to use Radical Inquiry, because it helps a group come together to voice their individual and collective aspirations. In this context, an effective evaluation design can ask:

▶ Who are we together? So what is important to us? Now what do we do to connect?

▶ So what is the current tension in the system? So what is the work and what are the impacts we intend?

▶ Now what can we do to set conditions for ourselves and others to create these impacts?

Because Radical Inquiry is a meaningful and transparent way to talk about coherence in a complex system, it makes it easy to see how things come together to create excellent performance.

STAR

The STAR Assessment is a tool that was explicitly developed to support Adaptive Action, assessment, and evaluation. It can be used as a self-assessment tool, as a team or an individual reflects on their own practice. It can be a method of continuous improvement as a group addresses its own strengths and challenges. It can also be a program evaluation tool to identify how conditions might be shifted to improve how a team—and its individual members—are able to improve their performance.

In individual assessment applications, you can use the STAR to address these questions:

▶ What are the strengths and challenges for the student in each arm of the STAR?

▶ So what is out of balance?

▶ Now what will improve the balance for this student and his or her team?

When considering ways to improve the performance of a program or project, the STAR helps you discern:

▶ What are the strengths and challenges for the program in each arm of the STAR?

▶ So what is out of balance?

▶ Now what will improve the balance for this program?

Whether you use it in informal reflection and dialogue or create a formal process to collect and analyze data, the STAR brings to the forefront the basic patterns that are necessary for effectively working with teams in leadership, learning, and healing.

Good, Better, Best

In Module 3: Find the Fix that Fits, you learned how to distinguish between Finite and Infinite Games and how to use Adaptive Action to lead effectively in both. This distinction, between low and high constraints, is very useful in both student assessment and program evaluation. Highly constrained, predictable patterns can be measured with precise, quantifiable indicators of performance. Unconstrained, unpredictable patterns require other kinds of assessment.

One more model will be helpful as you support assessment and evaluation programs that include both Finite and Infinite Games. It helps people see the current situation and assess how likely they will be to find good, predictive measures of success. Finally, it helps you facilitate a conversation with others, so that you can all consider what kind of assessment or evaluation system is excellent enough in a given moment.

The Landscape Diagram demonstrates the impact of constraints on a system. It gives you a "map" or picture of how those constraints influence patterns of stability, activity, and decision making across the whole system. (For more information, refer to Appendix 3.)

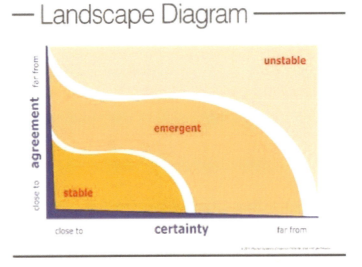

Figure 12: Landscape Diagram

Landscape Diagram: *Based on the amount of agreement among the members of a group and on the certainty of the environment, assess the current stability of the system (What?), the fit between current needs and current situation (So what?), and possible actions to make a difference.*

What? The Landscape Diagram helps you see, understand, and influence the conditions that create stability for individuals, groups, and communities.

So What? Under certain conditions, a complex system can be stable and predictable. Change the conditions, and it becomes unpredictable and unstable. A happy marriage can be stable for years, then a life crisis shifts it into patterns of instability. A team or organization can be reliable and high performing, and a change in membership, goal, or requirements make it unpredictable and unstable.

High stability can be a problem, too. When tradition stifles innovation, when habits interfere with health and wellbeing, when standard operating procedures interfere with good decisions in the moment, then you know your system is too constrained to do its work.

Now What? Use the Landscape Diagram to inform your Adaptive Action as you ask:

- ▶ Where are you and your system now?
- ▶ What position on the Landscape would be more productive?
- ▶ Now what can you do to change agreement and certainty to go where you need to go?

As a leader or educator in the system, you can use the Landscape Diagram to understand conditions that shape your ability to respond or take action or those that shape the overall responsiveness and adaptability of the system as a whole. Understanding the landscape around you informs your wise decisions as you respond to tension in the system.

In working on the Landscape Diagram, you constantly ask yourself whether the constraints at any given time allow for responsiveness and adaptability that is fit for a given function.

The two axes represent critical dimensions of human interaction.

The "X," or horizontal, axis represents the degree of certainty in the system. It describes a continuum from close to certainty (representing a high degree of predictability and stability) to far from certainty (representing little or no ability to predict how the system will behave and high levels of instability). A system that is close to certainty allows for greater control and clearer understanding of what is happening. The system is tightly constrained to minimize surprise. Constraints that generate high levels of certainty include close coupling, detailed specifications, limited diversity, small spaces or containers, and clear expectations. On the other hand, unclear specifications, broad diversity, ambiguous expectations, large spaces, and unclear connections are examples of how lack of constraint or low levels of constraint will push the system further from certainty and toward instability.

The "Y," or vertical, axis represents the degree of agreement. It describes a continuum from close to agreement (representing strong consensus and stability), to far from agreement (representing little or no commonality and instability). When agents are close to agreement, they see things in similar ways and respond to stimuli in the same way as other agents in the system. The system is constrained in such a way that disagreement is minimized or eliminated. Some examples of constraints that bring high levels of agreement include commitment to a shared goal, fear of punishment or retribution, clearly stated expectations, or high levels of similarity. At the same time, lack of clarity, freedom to challenge existing wisdom, ambiguous expectation, and broad diversity tend to push a system further from agreement and toward instability.

So What Can the Landscape Tell You?

Activities in a system can be assigned to one of three zones, based on levels of constraint. Given a particular situation, the two dimensions can be graphed according to the constraints in play.

Stable Zone – Close to Agreement and Certainty

This zone is predictable and constrained. Governed by procedure, rules, and policies, it is where organizational operations reside. One right answer to a multiple choice question, one best practice for a procedure, payroll procedures, employee supervision, and regulatory activities constrain a system to ensure employees know what is expected and can predict process or procedural activities to move forward.

A situation is fit for function here when reliability is high, processes can be repeated, situations are familiar, and outcomes are predictable and controllable.

Assessment or evaluation in the stable zone are based on predictable and controllable outcomes. Logic models, scorecards, precise measurements, and consistent processes are most effective in assessment and evaluation in this zone of the Landscape Diagram.

Emergent Zone – Further from Agreement and Certainty

This zone represents constraint that allows patterns to emerge. Constraints are strong enough to hold, yet loose enough to allow the system to respond and build fluid, robust connections. Examples of activity in this zone include learning, relationships, creativity, and innovation. Activities in the Emergent Zone are governed by Simple Rules that may be explicit or not.

When a situation is fit for function in the emergent zone, it is fluid and has the potential to change quickly. Examples of this kind of pattern in your work might include personal and professional relationships, chronic illness, emergency room processes, teamwork, public relations, and political advocacy.

In the Emergent Zone, outcomes and impacts cannot be predicted, so they are not good measures of performance. Patterns are emergent in this zone, so it can be helpful to track Pattern Logic, process measures, and levels of satisfaction over time to assess performance here.

Unstable Zone – Far from both Agreement and Certainty

This zone is characterized by disconnected weak signals that may or may not have meaning in the system. This zone has few, if any system constraints, so there are no discernable patterns. It is an area of random activity, unpredictability, and surprise. It is often where Research and Development personnel stand as they look into the broader landscape to explore new ideas, experiment with innovation, and seek the next niche.

We may not like to admit that patterns like this persist in our organizations and communities, but they do. And we are much more prepared to respond to them wisely when we can see them and support emerging patterns over time. Examples might include response to natural disaster, change in organizational or political power, or an unexpected shift in one's health or group wellbeing.

Assessment and evaluation in the Unstable Zone of the Landscape Diagram can be quite challenging. You and your team will encounter these challenges when judging performance in clinical settings or on complex collaborative or inter-professional activities. In this zone, exploratory evaluation methods can be most useful (Patton, 2011), such as tracking Adaptive Action cycles and observing changes over time using either quantitative or qualitative methods. Developmental evaluation can be particularly helpful here, as well.

You can use the conditions for self-organizing that shape Pattern Logic, to see, understand, and influence positioning on the Landscape Diagram. The figure below shows how the CDE Model influences and is influenced by the Landscape Diagram.

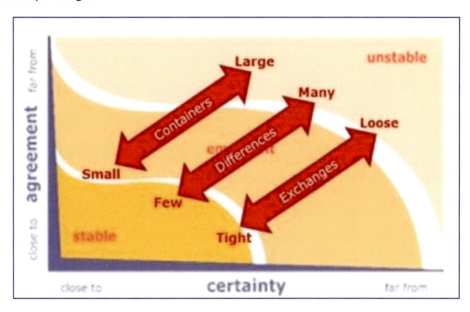

Figure 13: Constraints on the Landscape

4.2 Your Assessment and Evaluation Landscape

Reflect on these questions and share your thoughts online (less than 25 words):
- ▶ *What are examples of assessment and evaluation in Stable, Emergent, and Unstable Zones that you encounter in your leadership or in your teaching?*
- ▶ *So what assessment or evaluation systems have you found helpful in each? What are the challenges?*
- ▶ *Now what can you do to see, understand, and influence effective assessment and evaluation for your teams?*

When system constraints increase, activities move toward the Stable Zone. As system constraints decrease, they move toward the Unstable Zone. So, an institutional assessment or evaluation program should have the capacity to distinguish the levels of constraints and to adapt the data collection, analysis, and reporting processes to match the patterns of constraints in the system as a whole.

Now What Can You Do?

You can use the Landscape Diagram to see stability in a current situation, understand how it is or is not fit for function, and take action to shift constraints and change stability to be more productive. As you do, keep in mind:

▶ Any given map on a Landscape Diagram represents a single set of conditions. What is high constraint in one situation can show up as random or unconstrained in another. For instance, Company A may have done major development on an idea to create a new level of technology or product that Company B has no idea about. For Company B, those ideas are still highly unconstrained—individuals in that group are far from both agreement and certainty about the new idea. Once they become aware of it, they begin to constrain its meaning to them, moving it into emergence as Company B recognizes and builds on the new idea's use and/or value to them.

▶ Any given map may change across time or circumstance. As Company B becomes aware of a new idea, it begins to consider possibilities, opportunities, and limitations, relative to the new technology. Patterns begin to emerge as agents in the system move toward higher levels of agreement and certainty. Company B may like the new idea so much they decide to adopt it as their own. Then their work is to increase agreement and certainty in manufacturing or design.

▶ Any one individual's map on the Landscape Diagram depends on personal perceptions of constraint. Some individuals are more comfortable in the highly constrained, more predictable Stable Zone. Some individuals find their niche in the more fluid, connected Emergent Zone. Still other individuals love the surprise and lack of predictability of the Unstable Zone. One person is no more "right" than another. The question is about fitness. How do individuals contribute to the system at any point to allow greatest response, adaptation, and resilience? How do individuals best contribute to system fitness?

▶ By the same token, no one area of the map is better or worse than another. Where activities need to reside is solely dependent on where they best contribute to system fitness. There are activities that contribute to system fitness if they take place in the Stable Zone; activities that support best fitness when they reside in the Emergent Zone; and activities that are best fit for the Unstable Zone.

Technically, you have completed all the Adaptive Action Experiments that are required in the course, but we expect that you will continue to use Adaptive Action on all the Sticky Issues of your leadership life. If you choose to do one more formal Adaptive Action Experiment, you are invited to do it now. If you choose to do one, your optional Adaptive Action Experiment will give you an opportunity to use the Landscape Diagram to see and influence patterns in your own Sticky Issues.

> Students felt the need to reduce memorization and increase clinically authentic learning scenarios earlier in the curriculum of the medical school. The curriculum committee, with agreement from the faculty, moved to increase the participation of students in small-group learning and to decrease large group lectures in a medical curriculum. They limited lectures to two hours per day, added three, three-hour, small-group, problem-based learning group sessions per week, an afternoon of hands-on clinical skills sessions, and gave the students more free time during the day in the first two years of the new curriculum. The students were less stressed, enjoyed learning more and did equally as well on the examinations compared to those in the previously heavily lecture-based curriculum. The learning had moved from almost only replication in the Stable Zone to more inquiry-based learning in the Emergent Zone. What worked best was a mix of both kinds of learning.

Zones of Assessment and Evaluation

The Landscape Diagram has been widely used to design and manage large-scale evaluative thinking. It is particularly helpful when your decision making must draw on both quantitative and qualitative data sources, because it accommodates both easily.

Program or individual characteristics that are easy to predict and control, fit into the stable region of the Landscape. You can use traditional tests and quantitative measures of performance to make judgments and recommend action.

When using the Landscape Diagram to inform student assessment, consider the following questions:

▶ Where is the student now on the Landscape with regard to the knowledge, skills, and attitudes that are required?

▶ So what is most fit for function for the next stage of the student's development?

▶ Now what change in conditions will move the student toward greater fitness?

Program evaluation questions focus on the overall dynamics of the program as a whole. They could include:

▶ Where is the program now on the Landscape? What is the level of agreement? Of certainty?

▶ So what is most fit for function, considering the program objectives and intended outcomes?

▶ Now what change in conditions will move the program toward greater fitness?

Medical Education can be a 4, 5, or 6-year course of study. Adding in post-graduate specialization extends the learning further. During all these years, students are assessed hundreds of times. Formative and summative assessment is essential for learning and essential if we are to safeguard society and fulfill our social contract to produce competent and capable physicians able to meet the continuing needs of society. There is a wide and deep range of skills and applied knowledge required of students as they navigate through their medical education experience. There are well-established metrics for learning based on objectives (Bloom's taxonomy, 1956) and more recently in the recent revision of CanMEDS 2015 (Frank, Snell, Sherbino, 2015). The Landscape Diagram would be a useful way to show the range of assessments used by any given medical school. Some would be in the lower left corner of best practice with only one correct answer and very controlled situations. Others would be looking at variations and the ability of students to recognize them and choose the appropriate best practices. Putting students in authentic learning scenarios in various types of communities and clinics creates complex situations that have high validity, but low reliability.

Foundation for Judging Fit

We can talk about being physically fit or having a suit of clothes that fits, but what does it mean for a system to be fit for function?

It means that the system—individual, team, program, or institution—meets current requirements for performance. Even if those requirements are diverse and come from competing stakeholders, a system that is fit for function will be creative and innovative enough to adapt to what is expected. Even if the requirements change frequently and unexpectedly, the system will engage in Adaptive Action to see new demands, explore possibilities, make choices, and take action to respond to external and internal needs and demands.

A system that is fit for function does not just accommodate demands from outside, but it also responds to internal needs and expectations, including values, resources, expectations, and commitments. Health professionals who are fit for function are able to maintain their own wellbeing while supporting other professionals and providing excellent care to patients.

When something in a system—individual student, group, or instructional program—is not fit for function, there will be tension. That tension comes from a difference that is either under-constraining the system or over-constraining it. Consider the following examples.

▶ John is an intern working in the emergency room. He is constantly irritated and stressed. Nothing seems to be right. Others are sensitive and over-reactive around him. There is tension in the system. John is trying to control everything that is going on, and so he is over-constraining the system. That is not fit for function.

▶ The preceptor for Mary reports that she is unreliable, frequently absent, and sloppy in her documentation. This causes tension with her team and between her and the preceptor. Mary is under-constrained. That is not fit for function.

▶ A project plan was based on assumptions about access to time and human resources that would be necessary to implement a change. Over time, those assumptions did not prove to be true. The resources were not available, and the timeline was shortened to meet expectations of community partners. The project was over-constrained. That was not fit for function.

▶ Partners in a collaboration work well together during meetings, but they do not complete assignments and commitments between meetings. They are under-constrained. That is not fit for function.

As a leader, your goal is to influence conditions to help your staff, students, patients, and partners be most fit for function. You can use the idea of fit and constraints to see the patterns of current performance, imagine what might be more effective, then choose actions that are efficient and effective to make the good better.

Your Adaptive Action

As you consider your own Sticky Issues, you can use Interdependent Pairs to frame and respond to patterns in your systems.

▶ **What?** Identify and explore each pair separately. Use the information you have at hand to develop a deep awareness of where your group or organization falls on the landscape of change.

▶ **So What?** Clarify the impact of each pair on the others. Shift one of the dilemmas and see how it might interact with each of the others.

▶ **Now What?** Consider your options for shifting conditions and analyze the possible outcomes of your action. Then act, and watch carefully as you step right back to the next What? of your Adaptive Action cycle.

Adaptive Action

Our Adaptive Action

Throughout the course, we are assessing our performance and evaluating the course to be sure we meet your needs. Please help us continually improve this experience by providing feedback on how you are seeing the patterns we wish to create for you and your learning colleagues.

We use the HSD Simple Rules (in column one below) to guide our work in human systems dynamics and in the development, implementation, and evaluation of this course. After each Module, you will visit an online survey to capture your evaluation of your performance and of the course as you respond to these questions.

Simple Rule	I see this when . . .	I miss this when . . .
Teach and learn in every interaction		
Attend to the whole, the part, and the greater whole		
Give and get value for value		
Search for the true and the useful		
Engage in joyful practice		
Share your leadership story		

Table 9: Our Adaptive Action Module 4: Make the Good Better

Your Future Adaptive Actions

You are not required to complete a formal Adaptive Action Experiment in this Module, as the course is drawing to a close. We hope and expect that you have found the models and methods of Adaptive Action, Pattern Logic, Inquiry, and Simple Rules to be effective as you cope with leading in uncertainty. Continue to use these skills and share them with others over the coming months, and share your insights with your colleagues, students, and staff.

Health and Wellbeing

Throughout this course, you have had many opportunities to practice applying what you learn to support your own health and wellbeing. We hope you continue these practices that will help reduce your stress and prepare you to be resilient in the face of uncertainty and expanding expectations.

We hope you make a habit of reflecting on the questions below, sharing your thoughts with trusted others, and engaging in inquiry about how to create patterns of health and wellbeing for yourself and others.

4.3 Your Health and Wellbeing 4

Reflect on these questions and share your thoughts online, if you choose to do so:

▶ *What patterns emerge from your own, personal complex adaptive system? Emotional? Physical? Social?*

▶ *So what do you notice from day to day about how your patterns of health and wellbeing are the same? Different? Connected?*

▶ *So what are the tensions that inform your health and wellbeing at this time?*

▶ *Now what can you do in the next day to become more aware of and shift your patterns of personal health and wellbeing?*

▶ *Now what can you do today to influence health and wellbeing of your team and colleagues?*

Summary Make the Good Better

In this Module you have focused on the challenges and opportunities of leading evaluation and assessment programs in a complex, emergent, uncertain system. You have seen new questions you can ask, new sources of data you can collect, and new ways to be involved in continuous improvement for the learners you teach and the teams you lead.

Next What?

You, your colleagues, and your students face many complex challenges, and in the coming years those challenges will continue to increase in number and difficulty. To succeed as a leader and teacher, you must develop adaptive capacity. This course has been designed to help you see what is possible in complex environments, to understand your options for action, to take action, and to continue your learning and action cycles. In each Module, you have encountered new ways to think, talk, and act.

In **Module 1: Lead at the Edge of Uncertainty**, you learned about sources of uncertainty in your work place, community, and institution. You learned to:

► Define leadership as setting conditions for others to succeed
► Respond to challenges of leadership in complex environments
► Engage in Adaptive Action on your own Sticky Issues

In **Module 2: Work Better Together** you experienced opportunities to work across disciplinary and institutional boundaries. You practiced new ways to:

► Recognize the challenges and benefits of collaboration
► Engage with collaboration as a complex adaptive system
► Apply three promising approaches to leading in collaboration

In **Module 3: Find the Fix that Fits** you built your adaptive capacity to assess current situations, explore options for action, and move forward with your next wise action. You had multiple opportunities to:

► Define success in complex environments
► Practice Pattern Logic to see, understand, and influence others
► Use what you have learned in Modules 1 and 2 to find what is fit for function
► Manage stability and instability in your leadership context

In **Module 4: Make the Good Better** you discovered new and powerful ways to assess and evaluate, even when you cannot predict or control outcomes. With support from your peers and faculty you were able to:

► Explore multiple approaches to assessment and evaluation
► Use evaluation processes to inform learning and quality improvement
► Base assessment processes on principles of practice to integrate learning and performance

▶ Use systemic evaluation (Adaptive Action) to sustain patterns of successful performance

▶ Help your students, and those you lead, assess and improve their own performance

Throughout the course, you practiced what you learned in your Adaptive Action Experiments. While you learned, you also took action to shift your own complex system to be more productive, healthy, and effective. You are not only prepared to lead more effectively in uncertainty, but you also have the skills and knowledge you need to continue to improve your adaptive capacity over time and to complete Adaptive Action cycles to create conditions for others to be successful under your leadership.

Appendix 1: Models and Methods

This Appendix includes information about the HSD Models and Methods that are used throughout the LME course. For more information about these or other HSD concepts, models, or methods, visit the HSD Institute website at www.hsdinstitute.org.

The following Models and Methods are presented here:

▶ Adaptive Action
▶ Complex Adaptive System
▶ Finite & Infinite Games
▶ Interdependent Pairs
▶ Landscape Diagram
▶ Pattern Logic
▶ Radical Inquiry
▶ Simple Rules
▶ STAR

Adaptive Action

Description of Adaptive Action

Adaptive Action is an iterative, deceptively simple planning process that allows you to move forward in uncertainty. When you feel like you cannot move forward because you don't know what to do, you can always use Adaptive Action to identify your next wise action.

What? Using Adaptive Action you ask three questions. What? helps you name patterns of interaction and decision making that shape success. So what? helps you make sense of those patterns. Now what? helps you inform action to influence yourself and your team toward greater fit, success, and sustainability.

So What? In a complex world, you don't always see all that shapes the patterns around you. Adaptive Action gives you a way to see deeply into your world to understand the conditions that shape those patterns. You may work in an organization where the culture is toxic with competitive and hidden agendas. Adaptive Action gives you a path toward understanding the conditions that shape those patterns, and insights into potential actions to influence new patterns to shift the culture.

Every day you are challenged by "sticky" issues—questions with no answers. Problems that defy solution and recurring entanglements hold you in a limbo of indecision. Adaptive Action can move you forward by reminding you to look at the dynamics of your world to understand what is and to inform your next wise action.

Now What? Use Adaptive Action in your next Sticky Issue to:

- ► See the patterns in the challenges you face.
- ► Understand the dynamics that shape those patterns.
- ► Take wise action to more toward greater coherence and sustainability.

What is the Purpose of Adaptive Action?

Adaptive Action Planning is an iterative planning process involving three questions.

► **What?** – You gather pertinent data from across the system's environment to develop a picture of underlying dynamics of your current status.

► **So What?** – You examine data about those patterns to make sense of your observations and experiences. You use Pattern Logic* to develop an understanding of what the "picture" of your current status means so you can begin to explore and plan next steps. You explore the impact of the system patterns on the whole, part, and greater whole; the conditions that generated those patterns; and options for action that can shift the patterns to make the system more adaptable, more sustainable, more fit.

► **Now What?** – You take action and pause for a second check to measure your impact. By following up and asking where you are now and what is to be done next, you start the next cycle in the iterative process.

Progressing through the three steps to collect and analyze data that informs next steps becomes an ongoing cycle that can be carried out at all levels of the system. This sounds and looks much like the "Plan-Do-Check-Act"-type models that are used in a number of approaches to change. There are, however, fundamental differences that set Adaptive Action apart.

► What? So what? and Now what? questions use Pattern Logic to examine the dynamics of decision making and interaction. Analysis of patterns focuses on understanding the conditions (Containers, Differences, Exchanges) that make your issue so sticky.

► The connection between talk and action is quick and easy. Options for action emerge from what you see in the patterns themselves. You might choose to:
Amplify or damp current patterns by influencing environmental conditions.

Shape new patterns by shifting environmental conditions toward greater sustainability and fitness.

► This approach to planning is intended to be iterative and scalable:
Each cycle builds on the learning gleaned in previous cycles. Each "Now what?" returns to a new "What?" to launch a new cycle.

Each learning cycle can happen in the span of a heartbeat or across the arc of a lifetime.

Individuals, teams, organizations, and communities pursue their own Adaptive Actions at the same time. Together, they can create a coherent whole that is greater than the sum of the parts.

---

* For more information, visit www.hsdinstitute.org.

▶ Because Adaptive Action consists of questions, each cycle requires you to remain in a stance of inquiry, always watching, open to what you can learn from dynamics that swirl around you.

▶ Anyone can understand and use Adaptive Action. Children in kindergarten and CEOs of global corporations use these same simple questions to tackle their own intractable problems.

In a human system, long-range change can happen as individuals and groups use multiple and connected cycles of Adaptive Action to shape their own patterns of productivity and performance to support the overall, agreed-upon goals of the system. Engaging in Adaptive Action on an ongoing basis builds adaptive capacity, increasing your ability to be:

▶ Sensitive to your environment in a deeper and more useful way

▶ Responsive to the surprise and messiness of uncertainty

▶ Strong and resilient across the differences that shape your world

So What Can You Do to Engage in Adaptive Action?

Consider the one thing that is keeping you awake at night. Adaptive Action will help you see that challenge in new ways that, while not giving you a full-blown, ready to implement "answer," will help you see and take your next wise action.

What? In this phase of the Adaptive Action cycle, you are asking yourself what you currently know. What do you observe? What do you feel? What do you see? What are you hearing? What are you and others doing?

What can you learn from feedback and other observers in the system? Then there's the challenge: How do you make sense of all the data, information, and impressions that you collect over time? How do you stop the feeling that all that is swirling around in your head?

In HSD we use a process called the Pattern Spotters to support our Adaptive Actions. We came to this approach from Vygotsky via Bob Williams (http://users.actrix.co.nz/bobwill) This list of sentence stems helps you make sense of the patterns you see so you can move forward. When you have gathered the data, reflect on and respond to the following stems.

▶ In general I notice . . ..

▶ In general I notice . . ., except for . . ..

▶ On the one hand, I notice . . .. On the other hand I notice . . ..

▶ I was surprised by . . ..

▶ I wonder about . . ..

▶ This reminds me of . . ..

The responses to these questions will help you settle into the major patterns as they are playing themselves out in your world. This is one way to go from the messiness of emergent and unpredictable patterns into a more manageable description of the challenge at hand.

So What? At this point, you take the patterns you have named and use Pattern Logic to understand those patterns at a deeper level. Pattern Logic is the use and study of disciplined reasoning about the conditions for self-organization. In her ground-breaking research, Glenda Eoyang discovered three conditions that shape the speed, path, and direction of the system as patterns emerge. Using these patterns to understand your system and to take action is the essence of Pattern Logic. She has also found that those tensions in the system results from system fitness. Too much tension or too little tension in the system limits its coherence and resilience, decreasing its sustainability. As the system adjusts to find better fit, it will increase or decrease tension by shifting one or more condition. Change at any scale occurs when one or more conditions shift in response to tension.

Think about a balloon. At rest the air in the balloon is balanced with the air pressure in the room. The tension of the air molecules filling the space of the rubber "skin" of the balloon maintains the "pattern" we see as the shape, color, and size of the balloon. Over time, as air escapes through the microscopic spaces in the rubber of the balloon, it reduces the tension between the "skin" of the balloon and the air inside. The shape of the balloon changes as it slowly deflates into a pattern we recognize as a sad little piece of colored rubber with a sagging string tied to it. Another scenario might be that the balloon gets too close to a heater, and the air inside expands. Tension builds because the "skin" of the balloon is not adequate to hold the air inside. In a loud "pop" the rubber of the balloon is ruptured, and the air that was inside all escapes in a loud rush. This also releases the tension in the balloon, changing the pattern that we knew. This response to shifting tension and resulting changes in the conditions that shaped the balloon is a powerful metaphor to the ways patterns emerge and shift in human systems.

So what you can do, when you feel tension in your system that points to a lack of fitness, is to ask yourself where that tension is being formed. Is the container too large or too small? Are there too many differences? Too few? Are the exchanges fit for purpose in the overall functioning of the system? Those questions open many options for action and you can choose one. Choose the action that is easiest, or the one that's closest to you, or the one you think will have the most efficient impact. You don't have to shift all three conditions. They are so interdependent that a shift in one will shift the other two.

Now What? This is the point at which you:

▶ Take your most accessible next wise action
▶ Watch for the impact of that action.
▶ Return to the next cycle and ask "What?" do I see now?

Now What Can You Do to Shift Patterns Toward Greater Fitness?
First you take one small action and watch for the impact.

Plan that wise action:

▶ Who should be involved?
▶ What steps need to be taken?
▶ Who needs to know? What do they need to know?
▶ How will you judge/assess your success?
▶ When will you look for evidence?

Assess the impact of that wise action:

▶ Does the original pattern shift? In what ways?
▶ Is there more or less tension in the system? Is the tension more fit for purpose than before?
▶ As tension shifted one place, what was the impact in another?
▶ What, if any, unintended consequences or benefits do you see?

Look to the system to point you to the next cycle. Step into the next, **"What?"**

Complex Adaptive System

Description of Complex Adaptive System

This representation of a Complex Adaptive System (CAS) offers you a way to think about how patterns emerge from the complex interdependencies around you. Use it to inform understanding and action as you work to influence dominant patterns in your system.

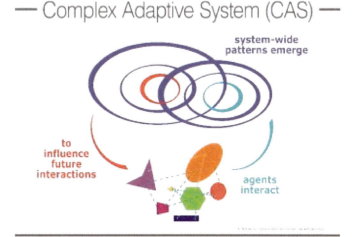

What? As early as 1997, Kevin Dooley, defined Complex Adaptive System (CAS) as "a group of semi-autonomous agents who interact in interdependent ways to produce system-wide patterns, such that those patterns then influence behavior of the agents." In human systems at all scales, you see patterns that emerge from the interactions of agents in that system. Thoughts, experiences, perceptions interact to create patterns of thought. Shared attitudes toward diet, exercise, and physical awareness interact to shape patterns of health in team or community. In an organization or business, individuals play out their roles, relationships, and expectations to generate patterns of competition or innovation. In organizations and communities, history, traditions, and expectations all influence behavior to shape dominant patterns we see as the culture of that group.

So What? Using this image of a Complex Adaptive System, you can explore your system on multiple scales, considering how agents' interactions generate patterns. It can inform your understandings of how some of those patterns emerge as dominant over others and how other patterns may be diminished and/or eradicated.

That level of access to underlying dynamics informs your sense making about what you see, experience, and know as reality in your team or community. You can understand why the competition is so fierce across departments in your organization. You can name the interactions that influence those patterns, and you can see how those particular patterns are a benefit or liability in the greater marketplace.

That level of access also has the potential to inform future action toward greater fitness for the whole system. If you recognize that internal competition is hindering your innovation cycle and creating slow response time in the market, you have a path to explore those patterns. You can consider conditions that shape those patterns and make better informed choices about your next wise action.*

---

* For more information, visit www.hsdinstitute.org.

Now What? Use Complex Adaptive System in your next Sticky Issue to:

▶ Visualize the interdependent agents that make up your system.

▶ Consider the dominant patterns that shape the culture or perspectives in your community.

▶ Explore current impact and potential influence in the conditions between and among the agents in your system.

What is the Purpose of the Complex Adaptive System (CAS) model?

A complex adaptive system (CAS) is defined by Kevin Dooley in 1997 as "a group of semi-autonomous agents who interact in interdependent ways to produce system-wide patterns, such that those patterns then influence behavior of the agents." This definition helps you visualize the dominant patterns of your team or organization and the ways the agents in that system—employees, departments, market factors, ideas—interact at all scales to create those patterns. It also enables you to consider how those patterns align with the landscape of the greater environment—the customer base, broader market, community values and interests. It allows both the short view and the longer view for taking action toward the best fit for your team.

In human systems, each agent (person, groups, and/or clusters of groups) has freedom to make their own choices about when and how they interact. That degree of freedom is influenced by a number of factors. Most specifically in a team, organization, or community, it is defined by dominant patterns in the greater complex adaptive system.

In organizations and communities, these dominant patterns are called "culture." In a small group or individual, they might be referred to as "personality." Ultimately behavior is influenced by those patterns, as people try to "fit in" with existing patterns. Tension is energy created when individuals work together to find the best fit with those dominant patterns. Sometimes it is the creative energy of innovation that moves a community to new levels of thought and performance. Sometimes it is the destructive energy of overblown competition and self-aggrandizement.

So What Can CAS Offer You?

The Complex Adaptive System model helps you identify and reflect on patterns, their fitness with the greater environment, and their triggers or origins in your own team. Patterns emerge as individuals and groups respond to tension in their environment, seeking coherence by adapting their own behaviors in response. Consider turbulence caused when two organizations merge. Employees find ways to clarify new expectations and take action to align themselves with the new emerging culture. In your social community, new members experience tension in the "different-ness" between their own experience and the dominant patterns they step into. Over time, they relieve that tension as they learn to fit with or ignore expectations of the greater group.

Some patterns are more productive than others, when considering sustainability and fitness. What helps someone reduce tension (find fitness) with their nearest neighbors in the system might increase tension (decrease fitness) with their greater community. For example, the behavior in a street gang is highly regimented, with clear expectations, hierarchies, and roles. To sustain participation (reduce or resolve tension) in such a culture often requires behaviors that put the street gang members at odds with the larger community, as manifested in turf wars, violence, and legal issues. Individuals and groups have to negotiate and navigate these differences in ways that seem most accessible to them at any given moment.

Because patterns in an organization are self-reinforcing, to change the "culture" requires individuals to change their behaviors on such a scale that they can influence existing patterns—amplifying those patterns they find productive, and damping patterns they find nonproductive. This is an ongoing and difficult challenge as individuals seek to shift shared expectations and agreements and generate new patterns. When you use CAS to visualize agents and their patterns, you are better able to identify conditions* they set in their interactions. Naming and exploring those conditions is a next step toward generating multiple options for your next wise action to change those patterns.

Now What Can You Do to Use CAS to Your Best Benefit?

Use CAS to help you visualize interdependence and emergence in your system. Use guides like Magic 21* protocol to help you identify the conditions being set by the agents in your system. Then you can explore ways to shift those conditions to influence the patterns toward greater fit.

- ▶ Name the patterns and identify the tension in those patterns—both the impact and the likely sources.
- ▶ Consider how interactions in the system do or can contribute to the tension.
- ▶ Engage with others to shift the tension and influence new patterns.
- ▶ See what happens and start the cycle again.

---

* For more information, visit www.hsdinstitute.org

Finite and Infinite Games

Description of Finite and Infinite Games

Finite and Infinite Games inform your decision making as you consider the long- and short-term implications of decisions and actions. In complex systems, it is crucial that you know whether you are making a decision, finding a solution, or taking action in a short-term, win-lose Finite Game, or if your actions and decisions are part of the longer-term, more sustainable Infinite Game.

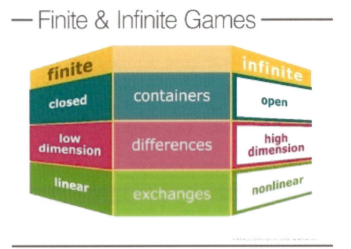

What? Some games are bounded and predictable, like baseball or basketball or bridge. You see the short-term immediate implications, and you play them to WIN. Other games, like marriage, productivity, and health, are unbounded. You see the long-term sustainability issues, and you play them to KEEP PLAYING. James P. Carse, in his book *Finite and Infinite Games*, offers a perspective that names the two and helps you know when, how, and why to play each kind of game. At HSD, we value both games equally, and help people know what it means to play each one well.

Finite Games have rules and timeframes. There are players, and there are observers in an established field of play. The rules for the games are set, and generally known by the players. Someone is designated as referee to judge how well you play by the rules. It is easy to see who wins. After the game, no one argues about the score. The object of the game is to get the highest score so you win.

Infinite Games, on the other hand, are more open and less defined. Everyone plays in an Infinite Game, and the field is not clearly defined. The rules of the game are not constant. They change all the time, and there are no external judges or referees. The players are accountable to themselves and each other for their behavior in the game. Ultimately, the rules of the game are devised to keep the game going—infinitely.

So What? While many models, methods, and approaches teach you how to play Finite Games, HSD focuses on strategies to thrive in the uncertainty of the Infinite Game. In 2013, Eoyang and Holladay described the nature of complex systems as being open to multiple forces, high dimension, and nonlinear. Those very characteristics make systems complex and call for the open, responsive, iterative nature of Infinite Games to set conditions for resilience and sustainability.

People, teams, and organizations engage in Finite Games to establish processes and procedures when certainty is necessary and possible. In uncertainty and chaos, people have to plan for and play Infinite Games. In fact, all Finite Games are played within the context of the Infinite Games.

► Arranging your schedule for a 30-minute walk each day is a Finite Game that contributes to the Infinite Game of lifetime attention and work to maintain a healthy life.

► Employee compensation and recognition of short-term performance goals are Finite Games that contribute to the Infinite Game of ensuring that employees are clear about their roles and the contributions they make to the organization's success.

► Household chores that are checked off the list each day are Finite Games in the Infinite Game of a relationship built on shared responsibility and respect.

Now What? Use Finite and Infinite Games in your next Sticky Issue to:

► Be clear about short-term and long-term outcomes, impacts.
► Understand the dynamics that shape the patterns of choice and behavior.
► Take wise action to move toward greater coherence and sustainability.

What is the Purpose of Finite and Infinite Games?

As our world becomes more complex—more boundless, more diverse, and more interconnected—we must learn to play a different game.

A Finite Game can be described by the usual sports analogies. There is a clear field of play. The game is bounded in time. There are consistent and well known rules, with some sort of referee or judge to ensure compliance. Players are clearly distinguished from observers; colleagues are distinguished from competitors. There is a focus on some way to keep score because the point of the game is to win.

Until recently these rules could work well enough for companies and organizations, for communities and neighborhoods, and for families and individuals. In business, consider an example of a hostile takeover. CEOs and supervisors created the game plan and gave others their instructions. The field of play was the market of competition or the courtrooms of negotiations. The games were bounded by time and financial constraints, or by market sector. The rules were set by external regulatory systems and watched over by lawyers and industry watchdogs. The players were the CEOs, other executives, and Boards of Directors, while employees, stakeholders, and customers were observers. Each "team" involved in the takeover was clearly identified, and the game played out until the winner either took over the other company or avoided being taken over. Whichever side wins, there remains the task of "cleaning up" the mess left by the game.

While that Finite Game might work for the details of such a deal, there are other factors today that call for another more Infinite Game that responds to the complexity of the twenty-first century landscape. In today's global economy, that level of merger in business calls for understanding of the Infinite Game:

- There are multiple fields of engagement, many of them not clearly defined, and a move in one field can have impact on other fields of play.
- The decisions you make and action you take are influenced by change over a long history or what is happening in an instant.
- Rules of engagement change often and unexpectedly and are context specific. No "one size fits all" engagements will work in such a game.
- Competitors can be partners, and partners can sometimes compete.
- Measures of success are many and varied, and constantly evolving.
- The primary purpose of the game is to keep playing.

When you consider that same hostile takeover, considering your actions in light of Infinite Games invites you to consider the long-term impacts of every move, to consider the strategy in a different light, and to pay attention to the risks and benefits you may be leaving in the wake.

So What Does It Mean to Play an Infinite Game?

Playing the Infinite Game requires a different set of skills, attitudes, and knowledge than those that brought you success in the Finite Games of the past. It requires you to build *adaptive capacity,* a unique and powerful ability to see the emerging and dominant patterns around you, understand those patterns in ways that inform wise action, and influence those patterns at all scales of your system. These skills include analyzing incoming information from multiple perspectives, using a variety of qualitative and quantitative tools, relying on both your rational and intuitive understandings to find your next wise action. Ultimately you have to attend to the system's response so that your next cycle of inquiry and action are informed by the outcomes of previous cycles.

Understanding Finite and Infinite Games reveals useful observations about playing in complex systems.

- You can play a Finite Game inside and Infinite one, but not the other way around.
- Communities are more likely to play Infinite Games than organizations are, because firms are usually bound by a corporate identity, focused on profits, and driven by more simple reporting relationships. Most communities have few if any of these constraints.
- Infinite Games rely on trust, courage, and adaptability, while Finite Games depend on strength, skill, and control.
- Human systems are always involved in Infinite Games, but sometimes it makes sense to play them as if they were Finite.
- Neither the Finite nor Infinite Game is better or worse—each is necessary in its own time. The only risk is playing one and expecting results of the other.
- Successful leaders understand the importance of both, and are skilled in both and are able to decide when each one is fit for function.
- The only way to thrive in an Infinite game is by Adaptive Action.

Now What Can You Do to Choose the Right Game?

Remembering that Finite Games and Infinite Games do not pose an "either/or" proposition, you have to know which game will be the best fit for the situation at hand. Is it a clear cut, unambiguous question of timing and organization? Then use a Finite Game to frame the action. On the other hand, is it a complex, massively entangled Sticky Issue that has you stuck? In that case, consider it as an Infinite Game and shift into the next **What?** by looking around you at the landscape you face. Find your next wise action to keep the game going.

Interdependent Pairs

Description of Interdependent Pairs

Interdependent Pairs is a model and method that allows individuals and groups to explore the paradoxes that emerge from the complexity in their systems. In a complex system, there is very little that is all or nothing. The challenges that have you stuck are the ones where there is no clear one-way consideration. The stickiness of your issues comes because you move on shifting landscapes between the extreme positions on the questions you face.

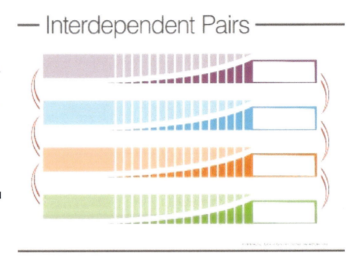

What? In our experience, unstable or unpredictable situations emerge from a framework of Interdependent Pairs. Examples include centralization or decentralization, long-term or short-term decisions, collaboration or independent work, optimizing the whole or the part. Barry Johnson, in his *Handbook of Polarity Management: Identifying and Managing Unsolvable Problems*, describes these pairs as polarities.

In a complex system, multiple polarities are at play at the same time, and they interact to make things even more complicated. Rarely do you operate at either extreme end of any pair. In less complex times, you could use phrases like "either/or" to describe a challenge or a decision. Then there was a recognition of the interdependent nature of some of these extremes in these polarities, and the movement was toward using "both/and" language. In highly complex systems, however, the more realistic picture is that the final critical factor actually lies along a continuum between the two extremes. The next wise action for anyone is dependent upon the unique factors present in a given situation. Additionally, in complex systems, another sources of uncertainty lies in the fact that multiple polarities exist and are interdependent with each other. A movement along one pair to resolve one challenge can lead to radical transformation along another pair and create new, unintended challenges.

So What? Leaders can use this model and method to explore the Interdependent Pairs that contribute to their own Sticky Issues. By looking at the dynamics of the patterns that shape their greatest challenges, leaders can identify the factors that are at play and the degree to which they influence each other. Issues like speed and quality make up one interdependent pair that any manufacturing leader has to consider. In today's competitive market, you cannot always afford to sacrifice quality for volume, but the tension always arises. Neither can you afford to take too much time creating the highest quality products. And it's impossible to have both! An item can be mass produced or it can be highly crafted over time. It's impossible for one item to have both. Another pair that challenges manufacturers is the idea of whether an item is intended for a single use or for longer lasting service. In issues of sustainability, this Pair becomes crucial.

So as a decision maker, you have to make a judgment about what is most fit for function at any given point in time. Mass produced, simple products that are for single use may not require the same level of quality that is required in an item that is intended to last a lifetime.

This is a pretty classic example of Interdependent Pairs, and it's relatively simple to consider. The challenge for you, as a leader, is to look more deeply into your system's Sticky Issues to identify the Interdependent Pairs that shape your challenges. Then, to use that understanding to inform your strategies and tactics.

Now What? So when you feel stuck in your next challenge—you cannot see your next step, use Interdependent Pairs as a model to help you see where you are stuck and as a method to help you identify your next step.

▶ What are the sticking points that seem intractable? Where is the tension in the system preventing movement? Which of those points seem to be in direct competition or contradiction to each other? Where and how are those points interdependent with each other and with other points of tension you see?
▶ So what can you do to find the balance between the Interdependent Pairs you see? What wise action will leverage the points to your greatest advantage?
▶ Now what action can you take to resolve the tension and move forward?

What is the Purpose of Interdependent Pairs?

Using Interdependent Pairs helps you see the relationships between and among the system tensions that keep you stuck. When you understand those relationships you have a better chance of using that tension to leverage productivity and performance across the system.

Here is an example from product development that represents this interdependent relationship among three such polarities. Effective product development efforts focus on dynamic relationships between:

▶ Quality and speed
▶ Quality and cost
▶ Cost and speed

It's simple to see how these pairs and their complex interdependencies could disrupt any simple plan for success. One decision might slide the product along the continuum from high quality toward low quality and increase along the continuum of speed. Slower production may enable higher quality, but it may also increase cost. When considered independently, any one of those decisions may be very difficult to make, but the interdependency with other pairs makes it even more challenging. The decision space becomes unstable because any single decision reshapes the relationships for all remaining decisions.

Finding the best balance in any such relationship is difficult. No simple formula will lead to that optimal solution. Trial and error that is based in deep understanding of the relationships between and among the pairs is the only viable strategy. That is why Adaptive Action is such a powerful tool in uncertain times because your decision making is grounded in understanding those relationships and allows for short feedback loops that increase your agility in responding.

So What Benefit Do Interdependent Pairs Offer?

Ignoring, misunderstanding, or mismanaging Interdependent Pairs is one of the easiest ways to get stuck in a complex human system. Whenever there is an apparently intractable problem, there is a good chance that some dysfunctional interdependent pair is to blame. Once you find the pair and agree on a way to manage it, the intractable problem resolves itself into a series of decisions, which may be difficult, but at least they are not impossible.

Every situation has its own unique set of most important Interdependent Pairs. Consider this example of pairs that you might encounter in your change efforts. These show up in a variety of ways, but the dynamics are undeniable. Large-scale, system-wide change is often complicated by a set of Interdependent Pairs that we call System Change Dilemmas.

Both ends of each spectrum offer risks and benefits. Traditional wisdom focuses on the left, while recent innovations in leadership and management support the right. HSD and Adaptive Action allow you to make conscious decisions to find the place along the multiple continua that is the best fit to situation and purpose. As a result, you access the benefits of both and minimize the risks of either.

Now What Can You Do to Use Interdependent Pairs?

While these systemic dilemmas are common across systems, there is still no one answer to the challenges they pose. Each system is unique; each dilemma carries its own dangers, surprises, and gifts. The most effective path is to use Adaptive Action in cycles of inquiry to see (What?), understand (So what?), and influence (Now what?) the patterns generated by each dilemma individually and among them all as they interact.

Engage in Adaptive Action, considering each pair independently, and then examine their impacts on each other.

- ▶ **What?** Identify and explore each pair separately. Use the information you have at hand to develop a deep awareness of where your organization falls on the landscape of change.
- ▶ **So what?** Clarify the impact of each pair on the others. Shift one of the dilemmas and see how it might interact with each of the others.
- ▶ **Now what?** Consider your options for shifting conditions and analyze the possible outcomes of your action. Then act, and watch carefully as you step right back to the next What? of your Adaptive Action cycle.

Landscape Diagram

Description of the Landscape Diagram

The Landscape Diagram demonstrates the impact of constraints on a system. It gives you a "map" or picture of how those constraints influence patterns of stability, activity, and decision making across the whole system.

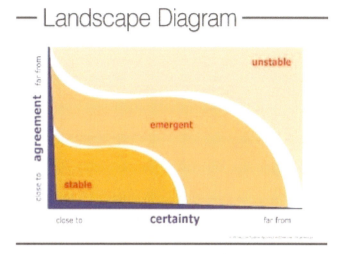

What? The Landscape Diagram helps you see, understand, and influence the conditions that create stability for individuals, groups, and communities.

So What? Under certain conditions, a complex system can be stable and predictable. Change the conditions, and it becomes unpredictable and unstable. A happy marriage can be stable for years, then a life crisis shifts it into patterns of instability. A team or organization can be reliable and high performing, and a change in membership, goal, or requirements make it unpredictable and unstable.

High stability can be a problem, too. When tradition stifles innovation, when habits interfere with health and wellbeing, when standard operating procedures interfere with good decisions in the moment, then you know your system is too constrained to do its work.

Now What? Use the Landscape Diagram to inform your Adaptive Action as you ask:

 ▶ Where are you and your system now?
 ▶ What position on the Landscape would be more productive?
 ▶ Now what can you do to change agreement and certainty to go where you need to go?

What is the Purpose of the Landscape Diagram?

As an individual in the system, you can use the Landscape Diagram to understand conditions that shape your ability to respond or take action or those that shape the overall responsiveness and adaptability of the system as a whole. Understanding the landscape around you informs your wise decisions as you respond to tension in the system.

The tension in the system informs your actions to increase or decrease constraints. For example, if data and information are not being used in a timely manner, you may find it is because one person or department is holding data. You look for actions to shift those particular constraints. Perhaps it is a lack of clarity about what needs to be shared—expectations are unclear. Your response could be to constrain those decisions by setting clear expectations about data sharing. On the other hand, that person may be hoarding information, releasing bits of information to a limited circle. In that case you can open lines of communication to increase the flow of data and the audience who receives it.

In working on the Landscape Diagram, you constantly ask yourself whether the constraints at any given time allow for responsiveness and adaptability that is fit for a given function.

The two axes represent critical dimensions of human interaction.

► The "X", or horizontal, axis represents the degree of certainty in the system. It describes a continuum from close to certainty (representing a high degree of predictability and stability) to far from certainty (representing little or no ability to predict how the system will behave and high levels of instability.) A system that is close to certainty allows for greater control and clearer understanding of what is happening. The system is tightly constrained to minimize surprise. Constraints that generate high levels of certainty include close coupling, detailed specifications, limited diversity, small spaces or containers, and clear expectations. On the other hand, unclear specifications, broad diversity, ambiguous expectations, large spaces, unclear connections are examples of how lack of constraint or low levels of constraint will push the system further from certainty and toward instability.

► The "Y", or vertical, axis represents the degree of agreement. It describes a continuum from close to agreement (representing strong consensus and stability), to far from agreement (representing little or no commonality and instability). When agents are close to agreement, they see things in similar ways and respond to stimuli in the same way as other agents in the system. The system is constrained in such a way that disagreement is minimized or eliminated. Some examples of constraints that bring high levels of agreement include commitment to a shared goal, fear of punishment or retribution, clearly stated expectations, or high levels of similarity. At the same time, lack of clarity, freedom to challenge existing wisdom, ambiguous expectation and broad diversity tend to push a system further from agreement and toward instability.

So What Can the Landscape Tell You?
Activities in a system can be assigned to one of three zones, based on levels of constraint. Given a particular situation, the two dimensions can be graphed according to the constraints in play.

► Stable Zone – Close to Agreement and Certainty – This zone is predictable and constrained. Governed by procedure, rules, and policies, it is where organizational operations reside. Payroll procedures, employee supervision, and regulatory activities constrain a system to ensure employees know what is expected and can predict process or procedural activities to move forward.

► Emergent Zone – Further from Agreement and Certainty – This zone represents constraint that allows patterns to emerge. Constraints are strong enough to hold, yet loose enough to allow the system to respond and build fluid, robust connections. Examples of activity in this zone include learning, relationship, creativity, and innovation. Activities in the Emergent Zone are governed by Simple Rules that may be explicit or not.

▶ Unstable Zone – Far from both Agreement and Certainty – This zone is characterized by disconnected weak signals that may or may not have meaning in the system. This zone has few, if any system constraints, so there are no discernable patterns. It is an area of random activity, unpredictability, and surprise. It is often where Research and Development personnel stand as they look into the broader landscape to explore new ideas, experiment with innovation, and seek the next niche.

When system constraints increase, activities move toward the Stable Zone. As system constraints decrease, they move toward the Unstable Zone.

Now What Can You Do?

You can use the Landscape Diagram to see stability in a current situation, understand how it is or is not fit for function, and take action to shift constraints and change stability to be more productive. As you do, keep in mind:

▶ Any given map on a Landscape Diagram represents a single set of conditions. What is high constraint in one situation can show up as random or unconstrained in another. For instance, Company A may have done major development on an idea to create a new level of technology or product that Company B has no idea about. For Company B, those ideas are still highly unconstrained—individuals in that group are far from both agreement and certainty about the new idea. Once they become aware of it, they begin to constrain what it means to them, moving it into emergence as Company B recognizes and builds on the new idea's use and/or value to them.

▶ Any given map may change across time or circumstance. As Company B becomes aware of a new idea, it begins to consider possibilities, opportunities, and limitations, relative to the new technology. Patterns begin to emerge as agents in the system move toward higher levels of agreement and certainty. Company B may like the new idea so much they decide to adopt it as their own. Then their work is to increase agreement and certainty in manufacturing or design.

▶ Any one individual's map on the Landscape Diagram depends on personal perceptions of constraint. Some individuals are more comfortable in the highly constrained, more predictable Stable Zone. Some individuals find their niche in the more fluid, connected Emergent Zone. Still other individuals love the surprise and lack of predictability of the Unstable Zone. One person is no more "right" than another. The question is about fitness. How do individuals contribute to the system at any point to allow greatest response, adaptation and resilience? How do individuals best contribute to system fitness?

▶ By the same token, no one area of the Map is better or worse than another. Where activities need to reside are solely dependent on where they best contribute to system fitness. There are activities that contribute to system fitness if they take place in the Stable Zone; activities that support best fit when they reside in the Emergent Zone; and activities that are best fit for the Unstable Zone.

How will you use the Landscape Diagram to inform your decisions?

Pattern Logic (CDE Model)

Description of Pattern Logic

Pattern Logic explains the three system conditions that influence the speed, path, and direction of self-organizing systems. The conditions shape the patterns that make up the reality of your world.

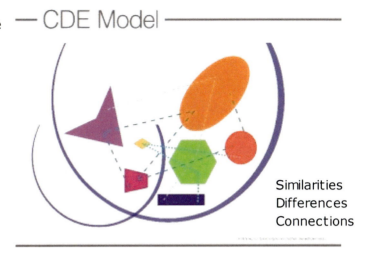

— CDE Model —

Similarities
Differences
Connections

What? Using Pattern Logic you can look deep into the dynamics of patterns around you. When you use this logic to explore the patterns in your life and work, you identify conditions that give rise to those patterns, and can speculate on how changing conditions can shift the patterns.

So What? The patterns that shape our lives—the success, the joys, the challenges, the opportunities, and just the patterns of everyday life and work—emerge as we move through the complex human systems where we live, work and play. These patterns are shaped by the interdependent influences of three conditions in those systems. The emergence of patterns is governed by the interplay among the conditions:

- ▶ **Similarities**: When things are alike, they tend to stick together and contain the system while patterns emerge;
- ▶ **Differences**: The significant distinctions that hold tension and have greatest influence on decision and action; and
- ▶ **Connections**: Relationships in the system that ensure the movement of information, energy, and other resources.

When you can explain the dynamics of your human systems at this level, in terms of what is same, what is different, and what is connected you increase the options to take wise action to influence those patterns toward greater coherence, resilience, effectiveness, and performance.

Now What? Use the Pattern Logic in your next Sticky Issue to:

- ▶ Understand the dynamics of the patterns that shape the problem.
- ▶ Identify options for action to influence those patterns.

Take action to change the conditions and bring about change, and then see what's next.

Radical Inquiry

Description of Radical Inquiry

Radical Inquiry is a process of reflection and exploration that helps you build system-wide clarity and coherence. As you become clearer about the patterns you want, you find ways to engage with others and your environment to set conditions to influence the emergence of those patterns. It's a process of looking deeply into the roots of a system to identify actions that can bring you to best fit.

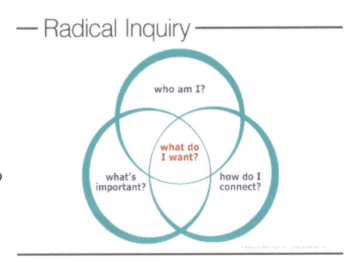

What? Radical Inquiry uses Pattern Logic to help you:

▶ Understand the patterns you want.

▶ Identify key conditions that can shape those patterns.

▶ Develop a short list of Simple Rules that can inform decision and action toward those patterns.

So What? Using Radical Inquiry brings a clarity of focus and an intentionality of language to help you align action and decision toward the patterns you see as best fit for you. Whether you complete the Radical Inquiry as a personal growth activity or you work with a group to design a shared Radical Inquiry, you agree on the patterns you want, create awareness about those critical patterns, agree on conditions that can shape those patterns, and commit to taking action that will set those conditions in your day-to-day actions. Radical Inquiry is a way of taking individual and/or group responsibility for performance and productivity.

Now What? Use the Radical Inquiry in your next Sticky Issue to:

▶ Declare publicly the patterns you want to live out.

▶ Identify the conditions that have the greatest chances of shaping those patterns.

▶ Create and follow a short list of Simple Rules that will shape those conditions in your life.

What is the Purpose of Radical Inquiry?

Radical Inquiry is a way to use Pattern Logic* to understand and explore patterns you want, to increase your awareness of conditions that will shape those patterns, and to define a short list of Simple Rules* that can inform decisions and behavior to set those conditions. It is a tool for self-reflection and planning, whether the "self" is you as an individual, a client in a coaching relationship, or a group that wants to build coherence as a team.

The name of the model and method is a key to understanding how it works. It is called "radical" because it aims for the "root" of your behavioral patterns. It is an inquiry because it calls you to stand in inquiry about what is and what is not possible in this time and place. In HSD we define inquiry in a very specific way. You are in inquiry when you:

▶ Turn judgment into curiosity.

▶ Turn disagreement into shared exploration.

▶ Turn defensiveness into self-reflection.

▶ Turn assumptions into questions.

You can step into this inquiry as an individual, with another as a couple or pair, or with a group or team. No matter how you engage with the work, it requires that you look at your world without judgment of right or wrong, good or bad, naughty or nice. What it asks is that you look around to see what would be the best fit in your space—at work, at home, in your community. What are the patterns that can sustain you in that space? What patterns indicate health and resilience? Then you move forward into the exploration, exploring with others, reflecting on your own participation and contribution, and questioning the assumptions that keep you stuck.

A Radical Inquiry is designed to help you shape the world you want—whether it's a family built on healthy relationships, a thriving community, or a first-class workplace.

So What Can I Do to Engage in Radical Inquiry?

The steps for Radical Inquiry are relatively simple. The challenge emerges as you go deeper into the implications of answering the questions honestly and clearly.

The first step is to name patterns you want to create. Start with the essence or the "sweet spot" of what you want. Refine that description down to a concise word or phrase that has particular meaning to you, and put it in the center of the diagram where all three circles overlap. That sets the tone and direction for the rest of the work. In a business context, that phrase can be as simple as *"Awesome customer service"* or *"Rule the niche."*

Then ask yourself what general, over-arching patterns will you see in your life, when you are functioning in that sweet spot. And in this part of the exercise, remember that patterns are not one-word descriptors like "Trust," "Confidence," or "Honesty."

---

* For more information, see www.hsdinstitute.org.

Single word descriptors help you know what's important, but it's hard to use that to inform your actions. At the same time, you cannot name every pattern that will contribute to your being "awesome customer service." Focus on 2-3 sentences that clearly characterize what you want and what it will look like when you get there. For example, if your "sweet spot" is awesome customer service, you might list the following sentences to describe what you want:

▶ Our customers trust our service and our products to serve their needs over the long haul.

▶ Our customers know they are valued and respected by every employee they contact.

▶ Our employees realize that anyone who receives services or products from them is a customer—whether that customer is a purchaser of our services or the fellow employee who works next to him/her inside the company.

Don't worry about wordsmithing here. The point is to capture the essence of the patterns you want to create. If you can agree on them, then the statement is good enough.

The next step is to consider the conditions that will shape those patterns, and what you need to do to create those conditions. A Radical Inquiry is based on three deceptively simple questions, shared by Leslie Patterson and her colleagues at North Stars Writing Project at University of North Texas. These questions align with the Eoyang **CDE** model* of conditions that influence the speed, path, and direction of emergent patterns. A **C**ontainer holds the system until the pattern can form. The **D**ifferences inside the container create the tension that gives form and shape to the pattern. The **E**xchanges are how that tension is shared across the system.

The following table describes the questions that Patterson and her colleagues named to help explore shared conditions.

---

* For more information, visit www.hsdinstitute.org.

Know the Conditions...	Explore the Questions...	Understand What You Are Looking For...
Container (C) bounds the system as the patterns emerge.	Who am I? or Who are we together?	This question forces you to consider your necessary stance, if you are going to live out that "sweet spot" you put in the center of your Radical Inquiry. Who do you have to "be" to live out the essence of your most desirable patterns?
Difference (D) establishes the potential for change	What's important around here?	When you identify what is important, then you can begin to focus on those differences that matter in your quest to achieve the essence of your most desirable patterns. You can look at the difference in degree (more or less of what is important) or difference in kind (one idea or focus is more important than another).
Exchanges (E) allow for sharing resources, energy, and information across the system.	How do we connect?	Consider the patterns you want to create to define how you will engage with your world. How will you explore, communicate, and connect to others to move toward the essence of who you want to be?

In the customer service example, you may say that the **C**ontainer that binds us together is that we are committed to being "Service in Action." The **D**ifferences that matter in your system could be about how you "Know and Recognize Customer Need." Finally, the **E**xchanges you would create enable you to see what people need and provide it. This could be captured in a phrase such as "See, Care, Share."

Your radical inquiry would look like this:

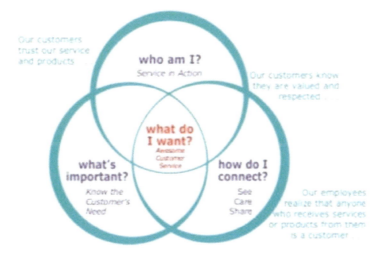

Now What Can the Radical Inquiry Offer You?

When your Sticky Issue results from a lack of connection, a Radical Inquiry will help you establish a path toward greater coherence. Because of the increased coherence across your system, you will notice that you are better able to respond to stressors in consistent ways that make sense. At the same time, increased coherence will enable your system to respond to opportunities in a more quick and flexible way.

In the example about customer service, consider the benefits that can result when the whole system is focused on improving all customer service.

- ▶ Your customers are more likely to remain loyal when times are difficult.
- ▶ Your employees are more likely to be engaged with each other and the work they do when they are treated with the same respect they give customers.
- ▶ Employees and customers alike are better able to rely on how they will be treated, wherever they access the system, because they see this as a systemic pattern.

In a highly competitive and changing market, patterns of this sort can help you build resilience and sustainability.

So when your Sticky Issue calls for increased coherence and responsiveness, take these steps:

- ▶ Declare publicly the patterns you want to live out.
- ▶ Identify the conditions that have the greatest chances of shaping those patterns.
- ▶ Create and follow a short list of Simple Rules that will shape those conditions in your life.

Simple Rules

Description of Simple Rules

Simple Rules are the agreed-upon guides that inform behavior and interactions among members of a Complex Adaptive System.* Whether by conscious agreement or by unspoken assent, members of a CAS appear to engage with each other according to a short list of Simple Rules. Those Simple Rules shape the conditions that characterize the dominant patterns of the system.

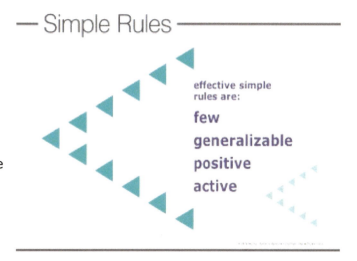

effective simple rules are:

few

generalizable

positive

active

What? Simple Rules can be overt agreements about behavior in a system or they can be covert understandings. They can guide the behavior of an individual or a team or a family or a community. Together the Simple Rules act in interdependent ways to influence the conditions that shape the speed, path, and direction of emergent patterns in the system.

So What? Because they shape the dominant patterns among the agents, Simple Rules shape the culture of a complex system. They can emerge from history of interactions and decisions, or Simple Rules can emerge in a short session of intentional planning and decision making.

Now What? Teams can use Simple Rules in a number of ways.

▶ They can come together and agree on the patterns they want and establish Simple Rules they believe will shape those patterns.

▶ They can review their work together retrospectively to identify the unspoken Simple Rules that may be in effect. Then the team can choose to continue with the Rules that shape patterns they want, and find new Rules to shape patterns they want to improve.

---

* For more information, see www.hsdinstitute.org.

What is the Purpose of Simple Rules?

Simple Rules are agreements that inform behavior, so a diverse group can function as one. They set conditions that shape the emergent patterns as a group self-organizes. The rules may emerge from covert or overt agreements among the players, and they inform decisions and actions to create coherence across the whole.

Families, organizations, and communities establish Simple Rules as they learn to live, work, and play together. Sometimes Simple Rules are codified through laws, regulations, contracts, or other formal means. At the same time Simple Rules can be unspoken, passing from person to person and generation to generation by the traditions and expectations that help people know how to belong and fit within the Simple Rules' cultural patterns.

The Human Systems Dynamics Institute uses a set of Simple Rules to define our culture—one that is aimed at ensuring resilience and coherence for individuals, groups, and our network as a whole. Employees, board members, network Associates, and interested colleagues around the globe experience these Simple Rules to shape the core patterns of the Institute. Our Simple Rules and their definitions appear below.

- ▶ **Teach and learn in every interaction** Stand together in inquiry, exploring ideas, building shared meaning, and learning from and with others. Share what you know and remain open to new ideas, deeper insights, and broader perspectives.
- ▶ **Give and get value for value** Build balanced relationships where each individual or group gets what is needed, and each is allowed to contribute as they can. Negotiate differences with questions that increase individual and collective resilience.
- ▶ **Search for the true and the useful** Ensure that solutions and questions address real-world complexity. Check for truth in what you see and hear; seek usefulness in what you learn. Question assumptions and subjective truths at all scales.
- ▶ **Attend to the whole, part, and greater whole** See linkages and connections across systems. Recognize forces and influences in all areas. While global issues shape conditions in your world, know that change is driven by person-to-person interactions.
- ▶ **Engage in joyful practice** Recognize the value of engagement and commitment. Understand how joyful practice emerges when individuals and groups engage in work they love, know their contribution to success of the greater whole, and know their contributions are valued.
- ▶ **Share your HSD story** Be explicit in your use of Pattern Logic to see, understand, and influence patterns. Use what you know to contribute to adaptive capacity in the systems where you live, work, and play. Share what you learn as you explore the options and opportunities of using HSD.

So What Can You Do to Use Simple Rules?

Simple Rules establish the conditions that give rise to patterns in the system. They can be covert agreements that emerge over time in a system, creating its culture. Often new leaders come into a system and state their intention to change the culture and "create a new world" for the workers, stakeholders, and customers. The problem is that unless intentional steps are taken to uncover and change the existing Simple Rules that hold those patterns in place, no amount of leadership command will change the system-wide patterns. Simple Rules can be used retrospectively to understand what shaped the conditions to generate whatever patterns are currently in the system.

On the other hand, Simple Rules can be used prospectively to shape a desired future. Groups can identify patterns they want to generate and define Simple Rules that seem most likely to help them generate those patterns. What is critical in establishing system-wide patterns is that everyone has to use a shared set of Simple Rules at all levels of decision making and action. This requires a shared understanding of what the Rules mean and agreements to use the Rules to make decisions.

Simple Rules are different from the norms we name for meetings and short-term interactions because they are intended to be more generally applied and not time bound. They are also different from values and beliefs because they are about action. They start with a verb, so they inform action.

Now What Can You Do to Create Simple Rules Do in Your System?

You can use Simple Rules in your system to shape the future.

- ▶ Name the dominant patterns in your system. Identify those you want to maintain and those you want to change.
- ▶ Work with others to develop a set of Simple Rules that will help to shape those patterns you want. Remember the rules about Simple Rules. They are:
  - ▷ Few in number (never more than about 7).
  - ▷ General statements that apply in any situation and to everyone across the system.
  - ▷ Always stated in the positive.
  - ▷ Always begin with action verbs.
- ▶ Find ways to embed Simple Rules in your own system. The following suggestions can help you do that.
- ▶ Discuss among yourselves what the Rules look like and what they do not look like. In systems where they have adopted Simple Rules, we work with different departments to explore what the Rules look like in their areas. We encourage individuals to consider what the Simple Rules mean to them personally and professionally.

▶ Take one each week to focus on in meetings and conversations.

   ▷ One CEO we worked with put one Simple Rule as a footer in her executive team agenda format. They talked about their work using that as a lens for that week. After having worked through the list, they used all five of their Simple Rules to asses and inform their work together.

   ▷ A department head formulates a question about the Simple Rules in every meeting, and each of the participants answers them.

▶ Write the Simple Rules on the wall. One of our clients has their list of Simple Rules painted as a mural on the wall in their Board Room.

▶ Put them in pictures, use them to tell the story of your system. Make sure they are shared across the organization. One kindergarten teacher we work with helped her students learn and use Simple Rules by using pictures, songs, and children's literature to help them understand patterns of behavior.

▶ Revisit the list often. As patterns become set in the system you may be able to shift to other areas to establish new Simple Rules.

▶ Don't call them "Simple Rules" if there are people who are bothered by the idea of more rules. One group we worked with called them "Seed Behaviors," and people were very comfortable stepping into their use.

STAR Diagram

Description of STAR Diagram

The STAR Diagram offers a way of seeing and understanding the conditions that shape a generative team. Whether you use it to plan for an effective team or to intervene when things go awry, the STAR diagram offers a way to see, understand, and influence the patterns in your team—at home, at work, or in your community.

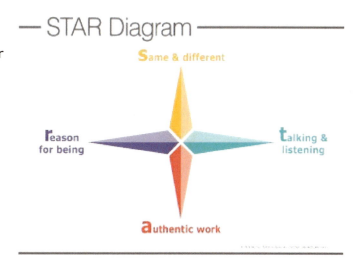

What? The STAR Diagram, initially framed by Brenda Zimmerman, represents four conditions that influence the nature of interaction and work in a group that comes together for a common purpose.

- ▶ **Same and Different** – Coherent, generative groups need enough similarity to hold them together and enough difference to create patterns and tension for energy and change.
- ▶ **Talking and Listening** – When people come together to accomplish a task, whether in the short term or across time, it's critical that each person is allowed to contribute and that each person listens to the contributions of others.
- ▶ **Authentic Work** – Teams need to do "real" work together. The challenges they face, the products they create, the opportunities they explore—all must be of real value to each of them and to the larger system of which they are a part.
- ▶ **Reason for Being** – Groups need a compelling reason for working together, both in short-term, periodic meetings, and in longer term of their overall purpose.

So What? Patterns of interaction and decision making in highly functioning, generative teams reflect a balance among all four points of the STAR. The conditions are balanced and functioning well. You can use the STAR Diagram in a number of ways.

▶ Assess current patterns to infuse energy into a team that has become stagnant or dysfunctional.
▶ Identify when a team has finished its work and is ready to sunset.
▶ Engage members of the group in understanding their own patterns and checking for balance among the conditions.
▶ Set shared expectations and commitments as a new team forms.

Now What? Use the STAR Diagram when you engage with teams/groups of all kinds to ensure generative, productive engagements.

▶ Define the patterns you have and/or the patterns you want.
▶ Discuss implications of those patterns for the individuals engaged in that team and identify actions that can set the conditions for the patterns you want.
▶ Engage with each other to set those conditions to build a generative team.
▶ Assess your progress regularly and adapt as necessary.

What is the Purpose of STAR Diagram?

The STAR Diagram, created by Brenda Zimmerman, provides a useful tool to support any group that works together toward a shared commitment or common goal. It provides guidance for groups that want to maintain generative relationships that are resilient and sustainable across the life of the team. In such a relationship, each point of the star is equal in size. When one or more point is out of balance, the group will struggle to sustain itself.

As a "model," the STAR Diagram offers a visual of the four conditions that can shape patterns of resilience and adaptability in a team, and it reflects the need for balance among those conditions. Each of the conditions is necessary in its own right, and it contributes to the effectiveness of the other three. It gives you a "picture" of what a highly performing, generative team looks like, relative to these four conditions.

▶ A balance of **Same and Different** ensures a diversity of thought and perspectives as you consider your work together.
▶ A balance of **Talking and Listening** means that all perspectives have voice in the decisions and actions of the team.
▶ **Authentic Work** says that the task of the group is meaningful and important to each of the group members.
▶ **Reason for Being** means that the group is together to accomplish something more than any of them could accomplish alone.

As a "method," the STAR Diagram informs your decision making and action taking as you explore your team's performance in each of the conditions.

So What Can You Do to Use STAR Diagram?

Given the dual purpose of the STAR Diagram, you can use it to ensure the generativity of your team. When you and your team members consider your shared performance in each of the points of the STAR, you can make judgments about where you need to shift your work together to move toward greater balance and fit. Where one of the "points" of the star falls short, you shift your interactions to bring them all back into balance. If you realize your work is complete or that there is no real reason to remain together, you dissolve the team to move on to other obligations and opportunities.

▶ **Same and Different** – Any group needs a balance. When too many similarities exist, the group's self-similarity prevents it from being stimulated to do work. At the same time, when there are too many differences, activity in the system cannot settle into a pattern. As you consider the members of the team, you consider their similarities. What commitments, interests, experiences, etc., are shared or similar among them? What diversity of thought, backgrounds, perspectives, and opinions do they bring? Are they similar enough to work together effectively? Are they different enough to explore new ideas and create new directions?

▶ **Talking and Listening** – Each individual needs to participate actively, even as they honor others' contributions. No one individual or group can dominate the conversation, and no individual or group can hold back, withdrawing from the work at hand. The reason for inviting diversity in the membership is to be sure that multiple perspectives are represented in decision making and action. If any of those perspectives are not granted voice in the work that must be done, there is no benefit derived from the diversity. At the same time, if group members only talk "at" each other, they don't hear the diversity of thought that could enhance their productivity or adaptability. As you participate in the work, are all perspectives given voice? Are the members of the team listening to each other, building on others' ideas and learning from each other?

▶ **Authentic Work** – Group members must feel their work is important and has meaning—it has to feel authentic to them. Often teams do "busy" work because they believe they have to accomplish something together, but they don't really buy into the work they are doing or they are unable or unwilling to contribute their best work. The work can lose meaning to the group. In a *Knowledge @ Wharton* article, "Putting a Face to a Name: The Art of Motivating Employees," authors point to research that talks about real engagement that comes from the chance to make a real contribution to work that has meaning. Work is authentic to the extent that it accesses the contributions of diverse, committed perspectives.

▶ **Reason for Being** – Similar to needing authentic work, group members have to believe in their reason for coming together. When they lose that, they no longer feel any commitment to the success of the group. There are times when teams finish the authentic work they have to do, but they continue meeting because they believe they should. Or a team or committee is formed without a meaningful reason—tradition, policy, procedural committees, for instance. Again real engagement requires that the members of the group know they are together for a reason that contributes to the success of the whole.

When you have explored your team against the points of the STAR, you can formulate a plan of action for setting conditions for generative work together.

Now What Can You Do to Use STAR Diagram in Your System?

After you and your team members understand what it takes to set the conditions for patterns of generativity, you can take action to take adaptive actions as members come and go, as situations change, and as opportunities emerge.

▶ Consider your patterns in a moment of time and evaluate the balances between and among existing conditions—**Same and Different**, **Talking and Listening**, **Authentic Work**, and **Reason for Being**.

▶ Understand the implications for what you find and identify options for action to address the challenges and amplify the strengths.

▶ Take action and watch for the impacts on the team's performance.

▶ Continue to function together, watching patterns as they emerge and fade.

Appendix 2: HSD IP Policy

The Human Systems Dynamics Institute has an open intellectual property policy. We invite you to use the Models and Methods you learn in this course to support your leadership and teaching, and we have two requests:

► Be sure to use citations for all HSD materials. You can reference the HSD website (www.hsdinstitute.org) if you do not have another specific reference.

► When you use the materials and alter them or learn something new, share your learning back with the HSD community of scholar practitioners. You can contact us at info@hsdinstitute.org.

Appendix 3: References

Setting the Stage

Eoyang, G. (2012). "*Human Systems Dynamics Paradigm Shift (v6)*". Online Resource documented 14 May, 2015.

Holladay, R., Quade, K. (2008). *Influencing Patterns for Change: A Human Systems Dynamics Primer for Leaders*. Createspace Publishing.

Holladay, R., Tytel, M. 2011. *Simple Rules: Radical Inquiry into Self.* Gold Canyon Press.

Eoyang, G., & Holladay, R. (2013). *Adaptive Action: Leveraging Uncertainty in Your Organization.* San Francisco: Stanford University Press.

HSD Institute. (2016, September 15). Rules of Inquiry {Web log post}. Retrieved September 15, 2016 from http://www.hsdinstitute.org/

Patterson, L., Holladay, R., Eoyang, G. (2013). *Radical Rules for Schools: Adaptive Action for Complex Change.* Human Systems Dynamics Institute Press.

Module 1: Lead at the Edge of Uncertainty

Eoyang, G.H. (2012). Sir Isaac's Dog: Learning for adaptive capacity. HSD Institute, www.hsdinstitute.org.

Fraser, S., & Greenhalgh, T. (2001). Coping with complexity: educating for capability. BMJ, 323, 799-803.

Goldberger, A.L. (1996). Non-linear dynamics for clinicians: Chaos theory, fractals, and complexity at the bedside. The Lancet, 347, 1312-1314.

Holt, T.A. (Ed.) (2004). Complexity for clinicians. Oxford: Radcliffe.

HSD Institute. (2016, September 15). Adaptive Action [Web log post]. Retrieved September 15, 2016, from http://www.hsdinstitute.org/

HSD Institute. (2016, September 15). CDE Model [Web log post]. Retrieved September 15, 2016, from http://www.hsdinstitute.org/

HSD Institute. (2016, September 15). Complex Adaptive System [Web log post]. Retrieved September 15, 2016, from http://www.hsdinstitute.org/

HSD Institute. (2016, September 15). Finite and Infinite Games. [Web log post]. Retrieved September 15, 2016, from http://www.hsdinstitute.org/

HSD Institute. (2016, September 15). Leadership as Fit Assessment [Web log post]. Retrieved September 15, 2016, from http://www.hsdinstitute.org/

HSD Institute. (2016, September 15). STAR Assessment and Handbook [Web log post]. Retrieved September 15, 2016, from http://www.hsdinstitute.org/

HSD Institute. (2016, September 15). Sticky Issue [Web log post]. Retrieved September 15, 2016, from http://www.hsdinstitute.org/

Kernick, D. (Ed.) (2004). Complexity and health care organization: a view from the street. Oxford: Radcliffe medical press.

Plsek, Paul. (2001). Redesigning health-care with insights from the science of complex adaptive systems. Paper presented at the Crossing the quality chasm: a new health care system for the 21st century, Washington DC.

Plsek, P.E., & Greenhalgh, T. (2001). The Challenge of complexity in health care. BMJ, 323(15 September), 625-628.

Rittel, H. W., & Webber, M. (1973). Dilemmas in a General Theory of Planning (Vol. 4). Policy Sciences.

Sweeney, K. (2006). *Complexity in primary care: understanding its value*. Oxford: Radcliffe.

Zimmerman, B., Lindberg, C., & Plsek, P. (2001). *Edgeware: insights from complexity science for health care leaders*. Irving, Texas: VHA.

Module 2: Work Better Together

Alfredson, T., & Cungu', A. (2008). *Negotiation Theory and Practice: A Review of the Literature.* EASYPol Module 179. Retrieved from http://www.fao.org/docs/up/easypol/550/4-5_negotiation_background_paper_179en.pdf Accessed August 4, 2016.

Covey, S. R. (2013). The 7 habits of highly effective people: Powerful lessons in personal change. New York: Simon & Schuster.

HSD Institute. (2016, September 15). Peace is a Pattern. [video]. Retrieved September 15, 2016, from http://www.hsdinstitute.org/

HSD Institute. (2016, September 15). Radical Inquiry. [Web log post]. Retrieved September 15, 2016, from http://www.hsdinstitute.org/

HSD Institute. (2016, September 15). Simple Rules. [Web log post]. Retrieved September 15, 2016, from http://www.hsdinstitute.org/

HSD Institute. (2016, September 15). STAR. [Web log post]. Retrieved September 15, 2016, from http://www.hsdinstitute.org/

HSD Institute. (2016, September 15). STAR Assessment and Handbook. [Web log].

Retrieved September 15, 2016, from http://www.hsdinstitute.org/

Marcus, L.J., Dorn, B.C., & McNulty, E.J. (2012). *The Walk in the Woods: A Step-by-Step Methods for Facilitating Interest-Based Negotiation and Conflict Resolution.* Negotiation Journal, July 2012, 337-349. https://github.com/emintham/Papers/blob/master/Negotiation%20Journal/Marcus,Dorn,McNulty-%20The%20Walk%20in%20the%20Woods:%20A%20Step-By-Step%20Method%20for%20Facilitating%20Interest-Based%20Negotiation%20and%20Conflict%20Resolution.pdf Accessed August 4, 2016.

Siders, C.T., & Aschenbrener, C.A. (1999). *Conflict Management Checklist: A diagnostic tool for assessing conflict in organizations.* The Physician Executive, July-August 1999, 32-37

Ury, W. (2007). Getting past no: negotiating your way from confrontation to cooperation. New York: Bantam.

Ury, W. *The walk from "no" to "yes" A Ted Talk on Youtube.* https://www.youtube.com/watch?v=Hc6yi_FtoNo.

Module 3: Find the Fix that Fits

Arrow, H., & Henry, K.B. (2010). Using complexity to promote group learning in healthcare. *J Eval Clin Practice*, 16, 861-866.

Cottingham, A.H., Suchman, A. L., Litzelman, D.K., Frankel, R.M., Mossbarger, D.L., Williamson, P.R., . . . Inui, T. S. (2008). Enhancing the informal curriculum of a medical school: a case study in organizational cultural change. *J Gen Intern Med*, 23(6), 715-722.

Goldstein, J.A. (1994). *The unshackled organization: facing the challenge of unpredictability through spontaneous reorganization*. Portland: Productivity Press.

Guastello, S.J. (2010). Self-organization and leadership emergence in emergency response teams. *Nonlinear Dynamics, Psychology, and Life Sciences Psychology, and Life Sciences*, 14(2), 179-204.

HSD Institute. (2016, September 15). *Leadership as Fit Assessment* [Web log post]. Retrieved September 15, 2016, from http://www.hsdinstitute.org/

Terry, R. W. (2001). *Seven zones for leadership: Acting authentically in stability and chaos*. Palo Alto, CA: Davies-Black Pub.

Module 4: Make the Good Better

Epstein, R. M., Dannefer, E.F., Jospe, N., Nofziger, A.C., Connard, L. W., Hansen, J.T., . . . Henson, L. C. (2004). Comprehensive assessment of professional competence: The Rochester experiment. *Teaching and Learning in Medicine*, 16(1), 186-196.

Frank, J.R., Snell, L., Sherbino, J. (eds.). (2015) CanMEDS 2015 Physician Competency Framework. Ottawa:Royal College of Physicians and Surgeons of Canada. Retrieved September 7, 2016, from http://www.royalcollege.ca/rcsite/canmeds/canmeds-framework-e

HSD Institute. (2016, September 15). Interdependent Pairs. [Web log post]. Retrieved September 15, 2016, from http://www.hsdinstitute.org/

HSD Institute. (2016, September 15). *Live Virtual Workshop on Interdependent Pairs.* [Video]. Retrieved September 15, 2016, from http://www.hsdinstitute.org/

Johnson, B. (1992). Polarity management: identifying and managing unsolvable problems. Amherst, MA: HRD Press.

Parsons, B. (2008, April 18). Designing Initiative Evaluation. Retrieved September 4, 2016, from http://www.wkkf.org/resource-directory/resource/2008/04/designing-initiative-evaluation-a-systems-orientated-framework-for-evaluating-social-change-efforts

Parsons, B. (2009). Evaluative Inquiry for Complex Times. *OD Practitioner*, 41, 1, 44-49.

Patton, MQ. (1997). *Utilization-focused evaluation* (3rd ed.). Thousand oaks: Sage.Schuwirth, L.W.T., & van der Vleuten, C.P.M. (2004). Changing education, changing assessment, changing research? *Medical Education*, 38, 805-812.

Patton, M.Q. (2011). Developmental Evaluation: Applying complexity concepts to enhance innovation and use. New York: The Guilford Press.

Schuwirth, L., & Ash, J. (2013). Assessing tomorrow's learners: incompetency-based education only a radically different holistic method of assessment will work. Six things we could forget. *Medical Teacher*, 35, 555-559.

Schuwirth, L.W.T., & van der Vleuten, C.P.M. (2004). Changing education, changing assessment, changing research? *Medical Education, 38*, 805-812.

Schuwirth, L., & van der Vleuten, C.P.M. (2011). Programmatic assessment: From assessment of learning to assessment for learning. *Medical Teacher*, 33, 478-485

Van Der Vleuten, Cees P. M., & Dannefer, E.F. (2012). Towards a systems approach to assessment. *Medical Teacher*, 34, 185-186.

Made in the USA
Middletown, DE
13 April 2017